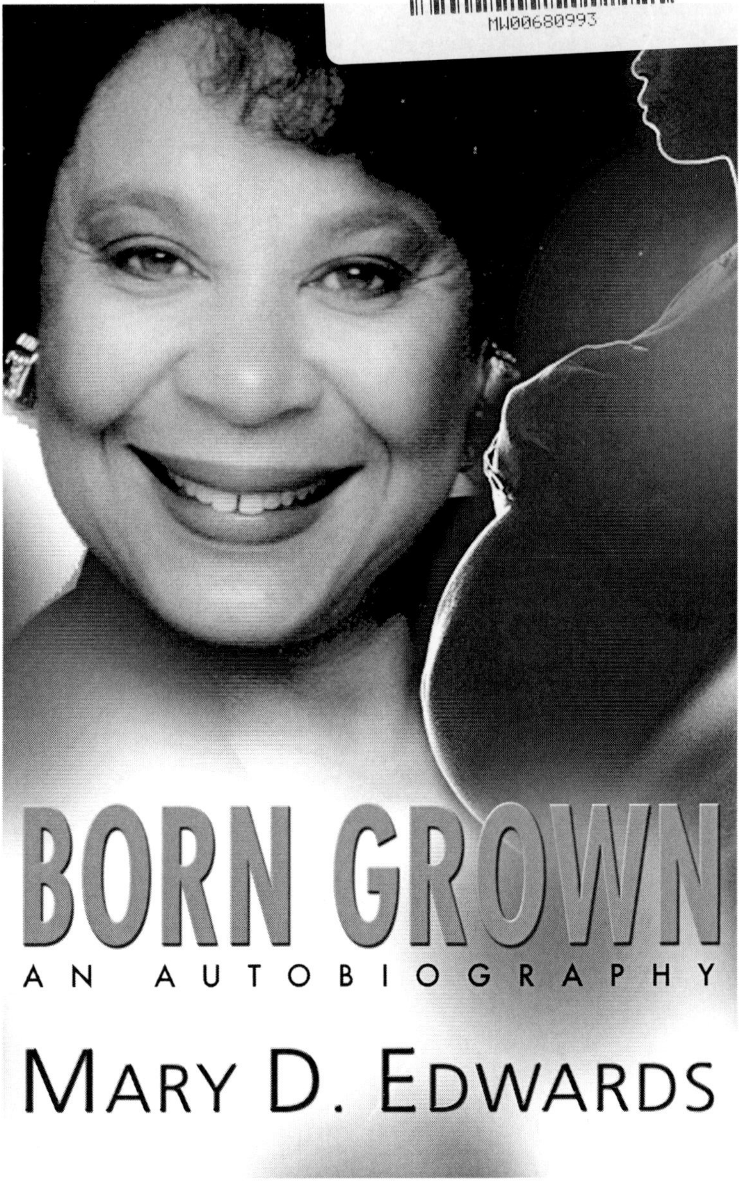

BORN GROWN

AN AUTOBIOGRAPHY

MARY D. EDWARDS

Detroit, Michigan

Born Grown

Take note that the name satan and associated
names are not capitalized. We choose not to
acknowledge him, even to the point of violating
grammatical rules.

Mary Edwards Ministries
P.O. Box 211018
Detroit, Michigan 48221
E-mail: edwardsmd@sbcglobal.net

ISBN: 0-9710482-4-X
Printed in the United States of America
www.borngrown.com
www.widowswithwisdom.org

Blessings
To Ward
& Single Point
Mrs Mary
Edwards
7-29-08

praise for

"Born Grown"

"As an author, I know it takes patience and perseverance to write a book. But to write a book as gritty, honest and self-revealing as Mary Edwards' ***Born Grown*** *requires another quality: courage. And Mary has courage in abundance.*

Hers is a courage forged by years of experience—tough, challenging, head-banging, gut-wrenching real life experience. Mary's take on life is not theoretical. It's practical and contains the kind of solid, down-to-earth advice that can only come from someone who's "been there."

From her heart-breaking account of a failed marriage, to her inspiring story of finding "Mr. Right," Mary shows an almost shocking willingness to reveal herself for the purpose of helping other "lost souls" find their way.

Above all, this remarkable book is a testimony to the power of God that can be unleashed in a human being willing to trust and willing to find the lessons in life's most difficult trials.

In every situation, Mary not only sees the glass as half full—she sees it running over with abundance. For her glass, clearly, is filled with the living waters promised by her Lord."

Mort Crim, Former Evening News Anchor
& Senior Editor, WDIV-TV (NBC),
Detroit, 1978-97

"I have known Minister Mary Edwards and her late husband, Rev. Eddie K. Edwards, for many years. Together they have been faithful pioneers in the city of Detroit for 30 years. I am pleased to see Minister Mary carry on, impacting the lives of the people God brings into her sphere of influence. Her autobiography, ***Born Grown****, is full of revelation. It will remove burdens, destroy yokes, and break generational curses."*

Catherine B. Eagan, President and CEO
The Wealthy Women
Kingdom Millionaire Training, LLC

"With authenticity, honesty, and courage, Mary Edwards has written a book filled with hope, encouragement, and a plan of action for living a powerful Christian life, no matter what negatives have been in your past. Mary reminds each of us that we were born for a purpose and God has a meaningful plan for our lives. Read Born Grown and buy ten more copies for people who need to know they are precious to God and they can use their life experiences as a platform of blessing as they reach out to others with truth and compassion."

Carol Kent, Speaker and Author
When I Lay My Isaac Down

Acknowledgments

Let me begin by expressing my appreciation to the many, many prayer warriors who stood in the gap for me during the time I was writing this book. Even in the midst of doing so, I had major family and health issues come upon me. There were times that I wasn't sure that I could continue. But, because of your faithfulness to intercede for me, I was able to carry on: *Wanda Burnside, The Called and Ready Writers, Debby Mitchell, Chaplain Omie Brooks, Marva Dozier, Evangelist Rosie Curry, Kelley Jackson, Stephanie Jones, Bishop Frankie Young, Deborah Jones, Deborah Walker, Martha Ricks. Shirley Reece,* and *Bob Kaczmarek,* my attorney, for giving me good advice as well as prayers. If you prayed for me and your name isn't listed here, please accept my apology and don't be offended. Whatever you do, please don't stop praying.

To those who endorsed this book: *Bishop Frankie Young, Minister Catherine Eagan Lt. Col. Clarence Harvey and Carol Kent.* Thank you for your vote of confidence.

To my editor, *Diane Reeder*. Thank you for getting into my heart and mind and asking me very significant questions, things that I hadn't originally addressed.

To my cover and interior designer, *LaTanya Orr,* who allowed God to use her even as she herself was going through family illness and challenges.

To my preliminary readers who took time out of their busy schedules to critique my manuscript: *Wanda Burnside,* president of The Called and Ready Writers and *Deborah Walker,* a former Joy of Jesus employee who remembered things that I had forgotten.

To my anointed cook, *Mama Minnie*. Thank you for making sure I ate nutritionally.

To my dear son *Donald,* for looking after me and driving me places I needed to go and not driving me crazy!

To my son in the Lord and neighbor, *Maurice Harden,* who gave critical computer support in a crisis.

To my many *friends* who supported me in ways not mentioned above.

Above all, thanks be to *God* for giving me the courage to write this very difficult family history. And for making sure my family and others benefit from it.

M.D.E.
"007":Mission Possible

Table of Contents

Although my mother and I loved each other, we never bonded as a mother and child should. Perhaps that's because she lost her mother at such an early age and missed out on a lot of the opportunity to be nurtured by her own mother, or by her grandmother who was not a good role model, either.

What I know about my ancestors is limited (as you will see in this book). I know very little about my maternal grandparents and less than nothing about my natural paternal grandparents. So much of what I do know, I wish I didn't, and would love to forget. However, I feel that I owe my children and my grandchildren what little knowledge I have.

It is my prayer that this "family history" will help my seed to better understand themselves, as well as me, and one day they will come to know Jesus Christ as I do: Savior, Lord, and Father. For it is only through His shed blood - a new blood line - can these generational curses be broken.

Minister Mary Darlene Edwards, Apostle

"But suppose this son has a son who sees all the sins his father commits, and though he sees them, he does not do such things: He does not eat at the mountain shrines or look to the idols of the house of Israel... He does not oppress anyone... He does not commit robbery, but gives his food to the hungry and provides clothing for the naked... He will not die for his father's sin; he will surely live. But his father will die for his own sin, because he practiced extortion, robbed his brother and did what was wrong among his people. Yet you ask, 'Why does the son not share the guilt of his father?' Since the son has done what is just and right and has been careful to keep all my decrees, he will surely live. The soul who sins is the one who will die. The son will not share the guilt of the father, nor will the father share the guilt of the son. The righteousness of the righteous man will be credited to him, and the wickedness of the wicked will be charged against him."

Ezekiel 18:14-16,18-20 (NIV)

Prelude

On April 28, 2001, the Lord blessed me to have a very successful writer's conference at Hope Evangelical Ministries in Detroit, MI. I had seen everyone on my team, every participant and every attendee, rejoicing over the breakthroughs, the learnings, the worship, the fellowship—it was a rich time, and as the leader of the event I should have been rejoicing with them.

Instead I came home, laid on my bed, and cried uncontrollably.

"Why am I crying like this?" I asked myself. The only answer I got was that I was sad. I was crying because I was sad. I knew that I was in big trouble. No more excuses. No more denial. No more faking happiness.

I slowly picked up the phone and called a psychiatrist that I knew. I began therapy for what he called "major depression." When he asked me how long I had been depressed, I responded, *"about a year." "No, dear,"* he replied, *"It's been much longer than that."*

After several therapy sessions, we concluded that I had been depressed since childhood, since about the age of 10. At the time, it had been nearly 50 years!

A couple of months later, on July 7, 2001, I read in the paper that Heinz Prechter, a very wealthy businessman here in Michigan, committed suicide. He hung himself. The headline read, *"A Life of Bold Vision and Demons."* The demon was the strongman of depression. Heinz Prechter's death brought about a kind of resurrection in my life, a great passion for writing that was quickly slipping away and close to death because of the same strongman.

While I don't understand a lot of the clinical aspects of depression, I do understand the emotional aspects. Growing up, I had been called *"moody"* or *"melancholy."* When I think back, I always felt a sense of sadness and dread. Always *"waiting for the other shoe to fall."* Very little peace of mind or happiness. Great fear!

The psychiatrist called my problem "a predisposition." The Bible calls it a "generational curse":

Those of you who are left will waste away
in the lands of their enemies because of their sins; also
because of their fathers' sin they will waste away.
Lev. 26:39

A survey of my family history easily supports this. I'm looking at the third and fourth generation of mental illness, which includes schizophrenia, bi-polarism, and attention deficit disorder, (ADD) just to name a few examples. And these are the family illnesses which have been only medically diagnosed! I strongly suspect there are other undiagnosed illnesses among our family.

Looking back at the drug and alcohol addictions in our family, I can see how family members have attempted to self-medicate, knowing that something was wrong but not knowing or attempting to find out what. I was in deep denial. I, too, had been in denial for years, blaming my sadness on a bad childhood, effects of a previous bad marriage, stress, menopause—anything to keep from facing the real issues.

As a part of my therapy, I was taken down memory lane. Won't you join me? There's something to be learned. When we know better, we do better. Those who don't remember or know the past are condemned to repeat it.

Introduction

We all know that what happened to our ancestors, to our parents, and to us, even while we are in our mother's womb, can have a major impact on our physical, emotional, and spiritual development. These events, these traits, are passed down to us and through us to our children and our children's children – generation after generation.

The one thing I know is that I was put on this earth to help break these generational curses. I know this because of my own personal struggles to break my own. This is my attempt, with God's help, to name those curses peculiar to my family, to help explain how the generational patterns have been passed down, and to take you along with me as we walk a victory walk together—a walk that continues well past the release of this book.

part one

In the Beginning...

Chapter 1

Eyes Like My Father

I was told I had my "father's eyes." I wish I had known earlier in my life how important it would be to share the eyes of my Heavenly Father.

"*You have your father's eyes.*" These are among the few words my mother could tell me about my father. I never knew my natural father, wish I never knew my stepfather and, in many ways, I grew up without a mother. In essence, I raised myself, my brothers, my sister, and I was a caretaker for my deeply troubled mother. I had no aunts, uncles, or cousins, no grandparents to provide the unconditional love that only a grandparent does instinctively. If I were I to describe myself in one word it would be "*Orphan.*"

This "orphan spirit" is debilitating. Ras Robinson, Founder and Overseer of Fullness in Christ Church in Fort

Worth, Texas puts it this way: *"You feel that you have no inheritance, no real heritage, no protection, no sense of security...and [no sense that anyone] really cares about your destiny." You have an overwhelming and foreboding sense of fear that the people who are caring for you—even if they don't do it very well—will abandon you. This feeling of abandonment is a pain beyond words, a companion to the orphan spirit. It plagues people whose father or mother walked away from them, for whatever reason. It plagues 'latchkey children,' or children whose fathers or mothers are either dead or who stay away from home because of work, divorce or other reasons." (www.fullnessonline.org)* Abandonment for me began in my mother's womb.

My mother, Audrey Gertrude Fountaine, was born in London, Ontario, Canada. Short and shapely, she took her height from her father and her nice figure from her mother. Mom's skin was as white as any white person's. She could have easily "passed," but never did. Her hair was naturally curly. And, even though she wasn't hard of hearing, you would often hear her say "Eh?" That seemed to be one of the favorite words used by Canadians. My mother and I resembled each other. When I look in the mirror, I see my mother's face.The actual date of my mother's birth has always been debatable. Her father, Edward Parde' Fountaine, a French-Canadian, says it was May 28th, 1924, but her mother, Rachel, says it was May 29th. Rachel was of Negro descent born in Canada. Her name was shortened to "Rae."

Mama never had her birth certificate, so she always

celebrated both of her "birthdays." If either day fell on a weekend, she celebrated all weekend long! She liked to have fun; I guess she got that trait from her grandmother Gertrude, her namesake.

"Gertie," as she was called, was known as a "party girl." Sadly, she enjoyed partying so much that she abandoned her children for the street life. One of Mama's most painful childhood memories was when she and her mother, my Grandma Rae, went to rescue Gertie's children. My great-grandmother Gertie had left them alone and hungry. Mama and Grandma Rae had to layer the children with their clothes because it was winter and they had no coats to wear outside. They eventually went to live with their aunt in Canada.

When my mother told me about that day, she said she remembered thinking, *"I would never leave my children like this."* Years later, she broke that vow. She didn't leave her children *"like this,"* but she did leave one behind. Abandonment would prove to be a family generational pattern.

Chapter 2

A Veil Over Her Eyes

Tell me, I pray thee, where the seer's house is.
1 Sam. 9:18b

I never knew my Grandmother Rae but did once see a black and white photograph of her. It revealed an attractive, tall, and large-boned woman. Looks like she could have weighed about 200 pounds. The family tells me that she was very shapely, with big pretty legs. In those days, cameras only took black and white photographs, but I'm told that she had coarse, naturally red hair. Interestingly enough, I've always liked red hair and started dyeing mine in my early teens.

My great-grandmother Gertie loved to party; hence, her nickname, "Party Girl." She lived a fast life, got pregnant at the age of 13, married, and gave birth to my grandmother, Rae, at the age of 14.

Grandma Rae married Edward Parde' Fountaine and had my mother, Audrey. I don't know much about my grandparents' married life but they had one other child, Arvine, who died as a toddler. He was accidentally scalded to death from a radiator that he touched while crawling around on the floor when no one was looking.

Grandma Rae didn't stay with my grandfather for long. She took my mother and ran off with another man. They also tell me that Grandma Rae had a "veil over her eyes." As a child, I never knew what that meant. But it sounded spooky to me when they said *"Grandma Rae knew things before they happened."* Years later I learned more about what that meant.

Tragedy seemed to run in Mama's family. When Mama was 14, Grandma Rae died giving birth to another child, who died when Grandma Rae died. I can recall my mother's sadness as she recounted the story to me. *"They carried your Grandma Rae and the baby up a hill in a wooden wagon to the graveyard,"* she told me. *"It was just before Christmas and a cold winter day, a day as sad as her death,"* she remembered. I have this vivid picture of the sad funeral procession. Even though I wasn't there, the sadness of the day remains in my soul.

Growing up, Christmas was always a sad time for my mother. Often times when we lose a loved one, we feel fear, anger and abandonment. Perhaps the lingering spirit of abandonment was what my mother felt. Maybe she felt all three.

Chapter 3

She's Leaving Home

All the rivers run into the sea; yet the sea is not full; unto the place from whence the rivers come, thither they return again.
Eccl. 1:7

When her mother Rae died, my mother went back home to her father in London, Ontario. Two years later, my grandfather remarried a woman named Lola. Mama and Lola didn't get along well at all. *"She was very dirty,"* Mama said. Lola had many black cats that climbed all over the kitchen table and got into the food. *"It bothered me,"* Mama continued, *"that Lola never washed her hands while she was cooking or after she played with her cats."*

One day Mama and Lola had a big argument about the cats. Mama called Lola's house a "pigpen," packed her bags and stormed out of the house. She was only 16 and had nowhere to go.

Mama became a high school dropout, during probably the last era when high school dropouts could still find their way in the world. Over the next two years, she worked at an ice cream parlor and had a room in a boarding house owned by Paul and Laura Lawson. The Lawsons were a lovely couple whom I once had the pleasure of meeting. They lived in London, Ontario, Canada.

It was at the ice cream parlor where my mother met my father, George Johnson, a Black American from Washington, D.C. who had joined the Canadian Mounted Police. George and Mama had a brief affair. Shortly afterwards, in 1941, the Japanese bombed Pearl Harbor in Hawaii, pulling the United States into WWII. George returned to the U.S. to fight for his own country.

After his departure from Canada, my mother discovered that she was pregnant.

Mama wrote my Dad, told him the news, and he promised to return to Canada, marry her and take her to the United States.

It would never happen. Mama was informed by one of George's military friends that he had been run over by a jeep and killed on the military base. Strangely enough, my mother never attempted to verify this story. I don't know why. Maybe she just didn't know enough at the time to even ask the right-questions. Maybe she was ashamed and embarrassed; after all, the culture at that time was much more ostracizing of unwed mothers, even those who planned to get married.

In any event, I never believed this story. But for some strange reason, I've always had a fear of being run over by a car, and I don't like driving either. My mother never learned to drive. And my granddaughter, Eboni, shares my driving fear. Fortunately, she eventually overcame it and has since taken to the road. When I asked her once how she overcame, she replied, *"You do what you have to do. I needed to get my baby back and forth to the sitter when I went to work. I didn't want to take him in the cold."*

Although I didn't believe the story about my father's death, I never asked too many questions in order to spare my-mother embarrassment. Besides, for many years, it didn't really matter to me who my father was. Ironically, my mother would always tell me, *"Girl, you need to study your roots."* So now, as I grow older, heritage becomes important to me. For the sake of my children and my children's children, we need to know.

Pregnant, her promised fiancé now apparently deceased, my mother made an attempt to come back home. As she slowly and fearfully walked up to the door, not knowing what to expect, what she got was another blow...

"You made your bed. Lie in it," her father said, perhaps feeling the sting of what was then seen as his daughter's

shameful condition. Eighteen, single, pregnant, scared, broke, homeless, and feeling abandoned and rejected, my mother sadly turned and walked away.

On October 11, 1942, on Thanksgiving Day in Toronto, Ontario, Canada, my mother gave birth to a 5-1/2 pound, blue eyed, blond hair baby girl–me. She named me "Mary Darlene." I was given her maiden surname, "Fountaine." She was 18.

Years later I asked Mama why she named me "Mary." She replied, *"Because the little Jewish girl's name was Mary, and she was soooo cute!"*

Funny thing is, Mama never liked the name Mary, and she refused to ever call me that. Instead, she called me *"Darlene,"* right until the day she died. Years later, I understood why. That's the name God wanted for me. I rejoice that "Mary" and "Darlene," mean, respectively, "Blessed" and "Beloved" in Hebrew. Even before I was in my mother's womb, my Heavenly Father was watching over me. My mother never knew that "Mary" is exactly the name God wanted me to have!

Later, Mama came back with me, her newborn daughter, in tow, begging them to take us in. They wouldn't let Mama stay, but did agree to keep me for a short period of time. I've always wondered why my mother let Lola, who she knew didn't like her, keep me. She probably didn't like me either.

Eventually my mother returned for me. Years later, I asked my mother how long I stayed. *"Not long,"* she told me. I never knew how long "Not long" was.

Years ago, with the little information that we had, my husband and I attempted to locate George Johnson, but didn't get very far. I never saw a picture of him, but my mother once told me, *"You have your father's eyes."* The only other information I have is that he lived in Washington, D.C., his family owned the Johnson Funeral Home there back in the 40's (now called the Johnson-Jenkins Funeral home), and that he was a medic in the U.S. military. We asked many questions throughout the D.C. neighborhood where he lived, but no one remembered George or his family. The funeral home has since changed names. We also wrote to the military, but with so little data to go on, we weren't able to get any information. No middle initial. No social security number, no known family. No goodbye.

Although she never said so, I believe this was part of the rejection syndrome that would plague my mother for life. That cycle started when her mother left her father, continued when she lost her fiancé, and when she attempted to return to her father's house with me in her womb.

Many years and five children later, Mama took us to the countryside of London, Ontario, Canada to meet our grandfather. The memories are not good. I remember a small, white man, sitting on a beer barrel in a yard, drinking beer, surrounded by old rusty cars, and looking at us like we were intruders.

Again, as it had done so many years before, rejection rears its ugly head.

Chapter 4

Nowhere to Lay

...the Son of Man has nowhere to lay His head...
Matt. 8:20b

Foxes have holes and birds have nests (Matt. 8:20), but my dear forsaken mother had nowhere to lay her head. Somehow she managed to find a family in Toronto to take her in, a Jewish family with a little girl named Mary. In exchange for childcare services, she was given room and board.

In 1944, when I was about two years old, Mama and I moved to the Lawson Boarding House in Toronto. This is where she met Phillip Bridgett, another African American. Phil worked for the railroad and rented a room at the boarding house whenever he passed through on his railroad job.

Phil was a big, dark-skinned man, a sharp dresser who always wore a hat and a big smile. I think he purposely grinned widely to show his ONE gold front tooth, of which he was very proud. Although he wasn't a handsome man, he was charismatic. More importantly, he offered my mother a "ticket" to the United States.

By the time Mama met Phil, she had just given birth to another child—a boy. Phil told my mother, *"I'll marry you and take you to the U.S., but you can only take one child."*

Len and Laura Lawson, owners of the boarding house, had been married for many years and longed to have a child of their own, but Laura was barren. They begged Mama to leave her infant son with them. She did. The spirit of abandonment had led Mama to do something she vowed she would never do – abandon her child. Again, history had repeated itself.

Leaving a child behind was heart wrenching for Mama. I know because the shame haunted her and she lived with her secret for many years. Mama was never one to cry easily. However, when she told me this story, tears fell from her eyes and she lowered her head. *"This has troubled me for a long, long time."*

The Lawsons changed the child's name to Paul and raised him in a loving home. Although Paul found out the truth years later, (none of us knew) he forgave Mama. He loved and accepted the Lawsons as his true parents. We never knew who his father was. When I asked Paul, he said that Mama wanted to tell him but he told her it didn't matter.

I'm happy to say that years later Mama searched for Paul and found him after the Lawson's death. By the time she found him, he had his own family. Mama told him the secret and brought him to the United States to meet us. We lavished love on him and his family. Today he calls me "Sis" and his daughters call me "Aunt." Paul still resides in Ontario. Mama was able to go to heaven in 1996 forgiven and in peace. I had the privilege of leading my mother to the Lord several years before she died.

I'm so sorry Paul got left behind. But I'm glad Mama took me.

To my dear brother, Paul:

Although you got "left behind," you were blessed to grow up in a much more stable home than the rest of my mother's children. Thank God for that! You were spared the domestic violence and all of the other emotional struggles we went through. God has had His hand on you, just as He has on me, from our mother's womb. This is confirmed as I read your recent correspondence to me. You are definitely a family man.

Yes, your wife abandoned you and the girls when they were very young. But you cared enough about them to try to keep them together despite the odds. I thought about you as I watched the box office hit, *"In Pursuit of Happyness,"* the story of a single father who also raised his son alone. He suffered some very challenging times, but succeeded and eventually became a multi-millionaire. You may never become a multi-millionaire, but you are richer than many who have done so.

You are a beautiful brother and one of my most responsible ones. I'm proud to have you as my brother.

Love,

Mary

Chapter 5

Coming to America

Children's children are the crown of old men...
Prov. 17:6

Although I was born on Thanksgiving Day in Toronto, Ontario, Canada, The United States of America is the only homeland I really know. My mother did marry Phil and he did bring us to the United States—specifically to Chicago, Illinois where he lived with his father, Cornelius. We called him "Daddy Pete."

Daddy Pete was once married to Phil's mother whom we called "Mama Lillian." They divorced many years before we came to Chicago and he had remarried a woman named "Mary." These two godly people had a son, Cornelius, Jr. Cornelius was wheelchair bound with cerebral palsy. In spite of his disability, he had one of the biggest smiles I've ever seen.

After all of these years, I can still see him grinning from ear to ear and attempting to verbally greet us. His feeble body radiated with excitement when he saw us.

There's not a lot that I can recall about my early days in Chicago. We got our own house and Phil was still working on the railroad. Mama had three more babies in quick succession: Sharon, Phillip, Jr. and Ronald. It seemed like Phil came home only long enough to deposit his seed!

I can remember some funny stories, though. One day my family was sitting around the dinner table with guests. I was about two years old and was walking around literally carrying a load—in my diaper. But no one knew it. Phil said I kept pulling on his leg for attention. But he kept shoving me away. He lived to regret it.

The next thing he knew I handed him something under the table in his hand saying *"Here Daddy."* You guessed it: a pile of poop. Talk about being a handful! Although I was too young to recall this scenario, they tell me my Daddy used his favorite expression: *"Aw Shit!"* He was right.

Kids Say the Darndest Things. Remember that show? Hosted by Art Linkletter in the 1960s, and in the '80s and '90s by Bill Cosby, the show focused on the honesty and innocence of kids. When I contracted the chicken pox as a small child, I probably could have been on that show. Phil and Mama left me at home while they went to the supermarket. They told me not to look out of the window because the sun wouldn't be good to get in my eyes with the chicken pox. As they proceeded out the door, Mama said, *"If you will be a good girl, we'll bring you something back. What do you want?"* My innocent reply was, *"A big black sucker like Daddy!"* They tell me everyone laughed. However, years later I heard my Mama call my Daddy that— and nobody laughed.

I was only three years old when my sister Sharon was born. Sharon's first name was Lillian, after her paternal grandmother, but we always called her by her middle name. Sharon was always very special to me. Now, I don't remember my first day of school the way many children do. But what I do remember is the day I lost Sharon, *"Hold your sister's hand tightly,"* my Mama said to me as Sharon and I were preparing to go to the corner store. The corner store was just a few doors down but on the opposite side of the street from our home. *"And when you get to the corner, leave her there until you come back. Don't take her across the street,"* my mother further instructed.

Although our mother loved us, in many ways she didn't have maternal instincts. In all fairness, however let me say that she was very young when she had us. She loved us but she made an honest mistake sending us alone to the store. In her defense, she had her hands full with four children under the age of seven years old. I was the oldest, very mature and helped her a lot with the younger children. But I was only seven years old. Sharon was four. We were being sent to the corner store to get a loaf of bread for Mama to make sandwiches for our lunch. Mama was at home with our little brothers Rickey and Ronnie.

Off I went to do a big girl errand with my little sister in tow. When we got to the corner, I followed my Mama's instructions exactly and left Sharon safely, so I thought, standing there waiting as I crossed the street to the store.

Upon leaving the store, I immediately noticed that Sharon was nowhere in sight. Needless to say, I panicked and began to cry as I ran home to report the horrible news to my mother. Sharon was missing!

Mama soon joined me in a state of hysteria and called the police. The police came, got the story, and hurriedly left to begin an intensive search for Sharon.

Hours later we found her. Obviously, her little chubby legs had climbed the steps of the neighborhood church. There was no one else around. But there was Sharon—fast asleep on a front row pew. All's well that ends well. God was looking out for her even then.

Phillip, Jr. was next in line. We called him "Rickey." Rickey looked like Phil had spit him out. He was definitely Phil, Jr.; just a lighter version. He took his coloring after Mama. And like me, he had blue eyes and blond hair. He was an eight-month breach birth baby (head first). Breach birth babies have to fight for survival. Often times, they don't make it. Rickey nearly didn't, and he's been fighting ever since. He's been sickly all of his life, suffering from respiratory problems, diabetes and gout. He is also a cancer survivor. But he has not always coped well with these struggles. Rickey is an alcoholic.

Chemical dependency started early with Rickey. One of my earliest memories of this is when I caught him in a closet hiding and sniffing glue. He was about eight years old. Rickey has spent most of his adult life either in jail or on the streets of Memphis, Tennessee. While many homeless people wheel their worldly goods around in shopping carts and bags, Rickey stores his in his cousin's outhouse! When he is sober, which is far too infrequent, my dear brother is very quiet and kind. He probably has more love for his family than most of us. Although he only had an eighth grade education, he is extremely skillful with his hands and once told me that he could build an entire house—except for putting in the electricity. I believe him based on the excellent work we have seen him do in our ministry and in our home. What a waste of talent. Alcohol has destroyed him and robbed him of his family and potential. He has children and grandchildren in Memphis. He has not been a good role model for them.

It is my prayer that Rickey will not die an unsaved alcoholic, but will come to know Jesus Christ as his Savior and be delivered from alcoholism just as his alcoholic father was before he died. I was blessed to be the one to lead him to the Lord.

Rickey was always Mama Lillian's favorite grandchild. Mama Lillian was Phil's mother and she lived in Memphis,

Tennessee. She was a dedicated Christian woman and I'm sure she prayed for all of us—especially Rickey.

After Rickey came Ronald, a.k.a. "Ronnie." We always referred to Rickey and Ronnie as "The Boys," even when they were adults. Unfortunately, they lived up to that name; they never grew up. Even though they aged, they never matured, acting like "boys" throughout their lives. History repeated itself, as neither brother raised the children they fathered.

Looking back, I can see where Ronnie was always an emotionally troubled child. The first year we went to Memphis to spend the summer with Mama Lillian, Ronnie cried so hard that Mama had to turn right around and come back for him. He was about three or four years old. Later, when he got to adolescence, he was short for his age, taking his slight build from his maternal grandfather Parde', and had a low self-esteem problem. Mama was concerned about his slow development and took him to the doctor for an examination and consultation. The doctor recommended hormone replacement therapy. Many years ago, this was strange terminology. I can recall her asking me what I thought she should do. I was probably about 12 years old; how would I know? We decided to wait and see if he would grow. He didn't. The wrong decision was made and it wasn't ever corrected. Ronnie never recovered.

Ronnie grew up with a love/hate relationship with Mama. When you hate your parent, how can you love God?

He became a "beer alcoholic" and lived alone and lonely.

He died alone and lonely, too. In March of 2001, I tried several times to contact Ronnie by phone to no avail. He was living in Mama's house; it was five years after her death. Finally, I had the police come and break into the house. He had already been dead for several days.

I believe Ronnie had a death wish long before he died. *"Ronnie,"* I asked him one day, *"if you could take one little pill daily which would allow you to live a healthy life, would you?"* He shouted back at me, *"No!"*

Ronnie died a loner, an atheist, and an alcoholic in Mama's house. He had become a sociopath, manic-depressive, and a very angry man. Angry at Mama for giving birth to him. Angry at the world. Angry at God.

The one good thing that came out of Ronnie's life is that he fathered a very lovely daughter, Rachel, whom my husband and I had an opportunity to raise for several years.

My memories of Ronnie are all very sad. Sometimes I wonder if he ever had a happy day in his entire life. I shudder to think that he didn't.

Steven, Mama's last baby, came from a different mold. More about him later.

Somehow, in between giving birth and raising children, Mama worked as a cashier at R.R. Donnelly & Sons, a publishing company in Chicago. Because of her mixed heritage, her skin tone, her fine, curly hair and proper speech, her employer thought she was white, even though Mama never tried to "pass."

One day my big, burly, black father showed up at Mama's job and that was her last day on the job. They took one look at him, learned that he was her husband, and fired her on the spot. Of course, that was before affirmative action and the Equal Employment Opportunity Commission.

Chapter 6

Run, Mama, Run

No child deserves to have an alcoholic parent.

When I was about ten years old, Phil (whom I didn't know until many years later was my stepfather) lost his railroad job. At that point, he packed us up and we moved to the Motor City, Detroit, Michigan, where he got a job with Chrysler Motor Car Company.

I can't remember Phil drinking before we moved to Detroit. Perhaps it was the stress of working on the assembly line. Whatever the case might have been, he turned into a drunk, and our lives became a nightmare.

While he managed to stay sober and quiet throughout

the week, and maintained his employment at the factory, he turned our weekends into hell on earth. Instead of bringing home his paycheck so that we could have the necessities of life, he would stop at the bar and blow his entire pay on alcohol and gambling. Then he would stagger home, kick in the door, cuss and fight our mother because no food was ready. We didn't have any food because there was no money.

Mama was a little woman, only about 5'3" tall and weighed about 120 pounds. Phil was over six feet tall and weighed well over 200 pounds. Mama was brave, or maybe it was her pride. She didn't want the neighbors to know what was going on in our home. With all of the commotion though, they must have known.

Every weekend, she would try to fight him back as the four of us children would yell, *"Run Mama, run,"* hoping that she would run out of the house to safety. When the neighbors could no longer stand to hear the cussing, screaming, crying and glass breaking, they would eventually call the police. After what seemed like an eternity, they would arrive.

Even now, it's amazing to think back and remember how quickly Phil could sober up when the police arrived. Because Dr. Jekyll so easily turned into Mr. Hyde, the police would leave him there...until the next weekend, when the abuse would start all over again.

We kids went through hell. I can still see myself balled

up in a corner trying to disappear when they started fighting. The boys would try to pull Phil off Mama. But they were so small and he was so big. The school psychiatrist told my mother that if she didn't get me out of that environment I would surely have a nervous breakdown.

Eventually my mother moved out of the bedroom where she and Phil slept and began to sleep on the pullout sofa with me. All night long I could hear him telling her she had better come in the room to bed with him or he would come out and kick her ass. And all night long she would beg me to stay awake so he wouldn't come out and hurt her.

Out of fear, I developed insomnia in my early years—afraid to go to sleep lest something would happen to my mother or other loved ones. It has taken years of therapy to be able to get beyond those childhood years and the trauma associated with them. I recall asking my mother once, *"Why do you put up with this?"* Her reply was, *"For you children."* What a poor reason. Her staying there was hurting more than helping us. All of us grew up fearful.

As children who didn't know any better, we were overwhelmed by shame. The shame of having fighting parents. The shame of poverty. I can still see those little notes in my mother's handwriting saying, *"Please lend me $2.00 until Friday so I can feed my children."* I had to take them to the neighbors in order to buy two hotdogs for Mama to make spaghetti for us – lest we starve.

No child deserves to feel shame and fear like that.

The day before my 10th birthday, on October 10, 1952, my youngest brother Steven Parde' was born. Mama and Phil had planned a birthday party for me on October 11th but Mama had to go to the hospital to give birth to Steven. When the guests came and found out the party had been cancelled, they took their gifts and went home. After that day, I always referred to Stevie as "my birthday present."

Stevie was my only brother who wasn't an alcoholic. He seemed to have his head on straight. Although he was born in Detroit, he spent his adult years in Chicago. He was keen on education and did a fine job of gaining knowledge. He acquired at least one master's degree. He taught physical education in the Chicago Public School. In his early 20's, he fathered a son, Steven Parde', Jr. We called him by his middle name, Parde', in order to distinguish from his father.

Stevie and Parde's mother Margie never married. But Stevie was a very good role model for his son. And, as I said earlier, he was from a different mold than my other two brothers, Ronnie and Rickey. He took on the responsibility of raising Parde' as a single father when his son expressed a desire to live with him. Steven raised a fine son.

I have very fond memories of my youngest brother. He was responsible and generous; he lent my first husband George and me several thousand dollars for a down payment on our first home. Stevie was also very attentive towards our mother. Although he lived in another state, he did more for her than my other two brothers who lived in Mama's home with her until the day she died.

My brother was not a smoker or a drinker and very much into physical fitness. That's why it was so strange to us when he died from a rare cancerous liver disease similar to that associated with heavy drinkers. It's the same affliction that took sports figure Walter Peyton's life in 2003.

It's an affliction that seems to run in the family. When Stevie died, he was the second family member we had lost in 18 months. Our family has been besieged over the years with cancer. Mama died on January 25, 1996 of lung cancer. Steven died on March 28, 1997. Sharon died on June 12, 1997 of lung cancer. Ronald died in March 2001 of liver cancer. Unlike Steven, he drank himself to death. My brother Rickey has been a stomach cancer survivor for more than 12 years. He is an alcoholic and hasn't stopped drinking yet. It must be his grandmother's prayers keeping him alive.

I have come to the conclusion that cancer is like the devil, or sin. It sneaks up on you, often without you knowing it, and takes over everything if it's not addressed. And like sin, researchers are now finding that the risks of cancer have a genetic component. In fact, there are certain genes that place your risk of cancer as high as 90 percent--even when environmental factors that cause the particular cancer only increase risk by a fraction of a percentage! As it turns out, lung cancer is caused more by environmental than by hereditary factors.

When Stevie died, I was so sick myself from various personal afflictions and from taking care of Mama and Sharon, that I was unable to attend his funeral in Chicago. I regret that. Some of my family members still haven't forgiven me. I hope that one day they will.

Chapter 7

Taking the Sheets to the Streets

Sometimes the best thing you can do for your children is to get them to safety. I honor my mother for doing that.

One day Mama hit "the numbers." Oh, what a glorious day it was! I can still see her sitting at our kitchen table counting stacks and stacks of money. I don't know how much it was, maybe only five hundred dollars, but it seemed like five million to us.

We had been washing our clothes in the bathtub, using a scrub board and laying the clothes on the radiator to dry. Mama bought a washer and dryer. I don't know if we had prayed about it or not, but that money seemed like answer to prayer to a poor family like us.

The joy was soon replaced with sorrow when Phil found out what Mama had done with the money. He jumped on her and beat her so badly that she could barely see out of her swollen eyes. She had a swollen lip to match.

For Mama, that was finally the last straw. It was the weekend and we knew he would be out getting drunk so she used that as our opportunity to escape the madness.

"Kids," she said, spreading two sheets in the middle of the floor, *"put what you can in these sheets. We're leaving."* I was nearly scared to death, but my joy overtook my fear as we hurried and put what we could in the sheets. It wasn't much, but we were getting away from this madman and that's all I cared about. There was a sense of relief we all felt as we took the sheets to the streets on foot. Mama carried our little brother Stevie, while the other four of us took turns carrying the sheets.

We spent the night with one of my mother's girlfriends who made it clear that we could only spend one night.

Shortly thereafter, we heard through the grapevine that Phil sold everything in the house, including the washer and dryer, for $250.00. He didn't waste any time.

We moved from my mother's girlfriend's home to an

empty flat. Yes, it was empty, but we were safe. That's all that mattered. I don't know how it happened. I never asked any questions.

Mama finally ran. She never looked back.

Chapter 8

An Honest Confession

Confession, even if it's about the people you love, can be a key part of emotional recovery.

This is not an easy book to write. More than once I've started and stopped: started because it's a story that needs to be told and stopped because I needed to seek therapy for some of my childhood issues that kept creeping up and interfering with my adult life.

I wish that I could say that I had a good mother. She did the best she could, but she was troubled, and we paid the price. I wish that I could say that she was a faithful wife. She wasn't. "Stevie," as we called him, the child Mama carried in the blanket when we hit the streets with the sheets, was conceived during my mother's marriage to Phil, but was not Phil's child.

Our little brother's father was a friend of our family. Although I will not attempt to justify what he and my mother did, had it not been for his help we would have been worse off than we were. To his good, this man provided food for us on many occasions when Phil had wasted the family's money on alcohol. To his bad, he was a deacon in his church and should have known and done better. He passed several years ago. I pray that he repented before it was too late.

In spite of what happened behind closed doors, I pay tribute to my mother. She fulfilled her assignment. She gave me a name, Mary, that she didn't even like; left her homeland, Canada, and made the decision to bring me to the United States where God has used me to fulfill my destiny and purpose. My mother's purpose was to get me here so that my purpose would not be aborted. That is what God is holding her accountable for. Deep in my heart I believe He is saying to Mama, *"Well done, my good and faithful servant. Enter ye into the joy of the Lord."* (Matt. 25:21)

Before she died, I had the wonderful opportunity to lead my mother to the Lord. She joined Fountain of Truth Missionary Baptist Church where she served as a nurse. Among her responsibilities was to aid those being prepared for and coming out of water baptism.

Chapter 9

Please Don't Take My Table

Sometimes, we honor our parents by NOT doing what they did.

After she left my father, Mama got a waitress job somewhere on Jefferson Avenue in Detroit. Over a period of time, we were able to purchase furniture. For a while, however, we slept on the bare floor. Mama cooked on a hot plate and we ate out of paper plates. But we were safe.

Our mother always kept a clean home. I can remember once living in a basement on Mullett Street in Detroit. We had carpet on the living room floor and, compared to some of our friends, we had one of the prettiest homes on the block, or if not the prettiest, certainly the cleanest! We couldn't afford a mop so we cleaned and waxed the floors that were bare on our hands and knees with Fels Naptha soap and a rag. The living room carpet was swept with a broom because we didn't have a vacuum cleaner.

Mama loved pretty things, especially furniture. I inherited that love from her. I would rather have furniture than a fur coat or a new car—really!

One time Mama purchased a lovely coffee table "on time," from the Good Housekeeping Shop. I can still see that little coupon book from which she made her monthly payments. Sitting in the middle of the round table was a globe-shaped glass container with a single red rose sealed inside. When you shook the container, artificial snowflakes would float around the rose. Mama was so proud of that table. It was one of the few possessions she had and it seemed to make her very happy.

That happiness didn't last long. Mama got behind in her payments and they came and took her table back. It's called "repossession." Mama was so sad. There are some generational curses that we succumb to, and others that we swear we'll avoid. I vowed that day that I would never buy anything I couldn't afford. I'm still that way today.

Chapter X

Born Grown

The most dangerous thing a mother can do to her daughter is fail to explain to her, lovingly and with great wisdom, the facts of life.

It was while we lived in the basement on Mullett Street that I began my menstrual cycle. I was 12 years old and about as ignorant as a young girl could be about the facts of life.

One morning I woke up from my sofa bed in the living room where I slept with my sister Sharon. Phil had come to visit earlier in the evening and had fallen fast asleep in a recliner. Mama had gone to her room to bed.

When I woke up, I felt something wet and sticky between my legs. I went to the bathroom to investigate. My pajamas were full of blood! I started screaming to the top of my lungs, *"I've been raped! I've been raped!"* I yelled hysterically.

Mama came running into the bathroom, surveyed the scene, and shook with laughter as she tried to explain. *"Honey, calm down. You haven't been raped. This is your period."*

"Period! What's a period?" I asked between sobs. My mother hadn't told me anything about periods or sex. But, if I knew anything about sex, no one told me that you would BLEED! I knew that I hadn't volunteered to have sex, so someone must have forced me. Mama explained to me that day about periods, but she didn't tell me enough. She didn't tell me about sex. She didn't explain to me that rape was definitely NOT sex. She certainly never connected lovemaking with real love, and how to realize the difference between lovemaking and sex. It would prove to be one of the greatest gaps in my understanding as a young girl.

Before my period, I can remember seeing in one of Mama's True Romance magazines a picture of a bride and a groom with the word "Sex" written across their chest. When I asked Mama what that word meant, she replied, *"You'll find out when you get married."* I found out. But I wasn't married.

The day I found out about sex I skipped school and went with a neighborhood boy to his home. His parents were away at work. He took me in the basement where his bedroom was. I thought we were going to watch television. How naïve I was. Before I knew it, he was all over me. When I resisted his advances, he threatened that he would find someone else.

My child-like mind told me that I didn't want to lose him. At the tender of age of 13 I got pregnant. It was the same day that I lost my virginity. I wasn't forced physically — but mentally. Although I was an honor roll student in school, I gave a wrong answer. I said 'yes' when I should have said 'no.' I don't recall any enjoyment. He wasn't around much after that.

"Are you pregnant?" asked my eighth-grade teacher.

"Yes." My answer was barely audible.

The full broomstick skirt that I had made in my home economics class no longer concealed my protruding belly. At the tender age of 13, I was six months pregnant and had gotten that way the same day that I lost my virginity. My teacher marched me to the principal's office.

It's been 50 years and I don't think I'll ever forget the expressions on my teacher's and principal's faces: a combination of sorrow and disgust. But even more so, I will never forget their penetrating words.

"What a tragedy. She's an honor roll student," my teacher said with tears in her eyes. *"And now all she will be is just another welfare statistic,"* the principal responded.

Their words pierced my heart like arrows and echoed in my head, adding judgment and anger to my already overburdened load of emotions: *"...just another welfare statistic."*

When Mama suspected I might be pregnant, she took me to the doctor for an examination. A single parent herself, with five children and two jobs, all she needed was another mouth to feed. When the doctor suggested that because of my age I should have an abortion, my mother asked me what I wanted to do. What a dilemma! I didn't want to be a mother, but the alternative seemed even worse.

My childhood hadn't been easy and motherhood would be even harder, but I made my choice. In spite of her deep and understandable disappointment, Mama said, *"Well, we are going to have a baby!"* She supported me – no matter what! Mama was only 31-years old at the time.

Graduation Day was only a few short weeks away, but it was the '50s, and I wouldn't walk across the stage to receive my diploma. My visit to the principal's office was my last day at school. I was told to pack my things and leave. My mother was called to pick me up from school. I walked away with a hung down head and a heavy heart. On a brighter note, my elementary school diploma, along with honor roll and achievement certificates, was mailed to my home.

On August 31, 1956, my son, Darrell Edward Bridgett, was born at Herman Kiefer Hospital in Detroit, Michigan. He took my last name. I had taken Phil's last name, "Bridgett," years before, although he never adopted me. Why? I don't know. As a matter of fact, I didn't find out that Phil wasn't my natural father until I was about 10 years old. The way that I found out was when he and Mama were in the midst of one of their violent arguments. I can't remember any of the details now. At some point, he reminded my mother that he was not my father. I recall a great feeling of relief. It was better to me not to have a father than to have one who was an alcoholic, wife beater, and one who put fear in the hearts of his children.

Darrell weighed in at 5-1/2 lbs. He was a beautiful brown baby with lots and lots of hair. In spite of my young age, my pregnancy wasn't especially hard. With the exception of labor pains in the maternity ward, I had an easy pregnancy. My mother tried her best to get into the delivery room but they kept her out. However, the delivery room was on the first floor of the hospital and I could hear her outside of the window saying. *"It's going to be okay, baby. It's going to be okay. Mama's here."*

His father was nowhere to be found.

I regret to say that my son has aged but he hasn't grown up. Most of his life he has struggled with one emotional problem after another. I must take responsibility for some of them. Being such a young mother, I made many mistakes. More later on that.

Many years later, after I had become "Minister Mary Edwards," I said to the Lord, *"I've missed my entire childhood." The Lord responded to me by saying, "So did Adam and Eve. They were born grown for a purpose. So were you."* I have since come to understand what that means.

Chapter 11

High School Daze

My "born grown" status was most evident in high school. I would later find that many, like me, had to face adult responsibilities as teenagers.

My son Darrell was born August 31,1956. School started back in September, and I entered Northwestern High School.

My high school days are a fading memory and mostly uneventful. Because I had responsibilities to take care of at home, including five children, four of them belonging to my mother and one of my own, I didn't participate in any after-school activities.

Reading became my only enjoyment. This was to my advantage. As a result, I spent time studying my schoolwork and excelled. When I was in the tenth grade, I received a double promotion, which enabled me to graduate early from the 12th grade with honors. I was 16 years old and the mother of a three-year-old son.

My honors were in business education classes, which was a good thing. Back in the 50's, scholarships to college were rare. If you didn't have money, you pursued business courses – not the university.

I didn't attend my senior prom because I didn't have a date. But that was okay with me. My mother and her latest boyfriend, Steve, took me to the Top Hat Restaurant in Windsor, Ontario, Canada, just across the border from Detroit. I had my first taste of frog legs and enjoyed them immensely.

Following graduation, I attended Detroit Business Institute until a thief stole my tuition money, which I accidentally left in my coat pocket in the school's closet. My mother was so disappointed. She really wanted me to finish business school.

Steve was a Polish man who was very good to Mama and us kids. He really loved Mama and wanted to marry her, but he was at least 20 years older than Mama and she felt he was too old for her. Steve was a widower.

One time he took us to his home in Grosse Pointe Woods, Michigan, a very affluent community. I'll never forget how he sneaked us through the backdoor of his home after the sun had gone down. Steve's home looked like a mansion to us. It was the most beautiful home we had ever seen. Steve's late wife had been an invalid and he had installed a special chair in his home for her to get from floor to floor. My brothers, sister and I had a great time taking turns riding in the chair. It felt like a day at the amusement park to us. Before we left, Steve roasted Polish sausages for us.

Some time later, Steve bought my mother a beautiful fur coat and bought us kids a television set. These items later cost us more than they were worth. Over a period of time, Steve stopped coming around. I don't know who quit whom, but Steve was no longer in the picture. After that, Mama lost her job and had to go on welfare. Those were the days when the social workers made surprise visits to your home. She made one to ours. When she inspected the premises, she didn't find a man. What she found was Mama's fur coat and our television set. These were considered "contraband" for folks on welfare. As a result, we were eliminated from the welfare rolls, and once again experienced a kind of rejection.

No job; no money; no place to live. No husband; no father; no choice. Mama packed us up to return to our grandparent's home in Chicago.

Chapter 12

Going To Chicago ...Again

Like attracts like...for better, or worse.

People are attracted to like spirits. When your own life is sad, you must be aware that you will be drawn to sad people, and you will have to make a special effort to reach out to people who have a more balanced perspective and a more positive spirit. I didn't do this. I was young and foolish. Instead, as the saying goes, "misery loves company." I was drawn to George Brooks like a magnet.

Right after high school I started dating him. Interestingly, he had the same first name as the father I never knew. George was the older brother of my girlfriend Roberta, aka "Bert." She and I were classmates and sat near each other because our surnames both started with "B."

George was 21 and had just returned from the Air Force when we met. I noticed him one day when I visited Bert. He was stretched out on a sofa listening to jazz saxophonist Miles Davis playing "Moody Blues." I don't recall what he was wearing, but I do remember thinking, *"Boy, he sure is skinny,"* His eyes were closed and he looked like he was in a world of his own.

George seemed to be such a sad man, very quiet, and a loner. I have always had an affinity for sad people, so I was drawn to him. We started dating just before Mama was cut off of welfare. As a result of being removed from the welfare rolls, we were unable to pay the rent and got evicted. Mama had to sell our furniture in order for us to have money to eat.

Penniless and homeless, we were on the road again to our grandfather, Daddy Pete's, home in Chicago. It was a crowded apartment and we were bursting out at the seams.

Although Mama abandoned Paul in Canada, over the years she took in many children who were not her own. This included my sister Sharon's best girlfriend, Doris Griffin. Today, Doris pastors' The Full Armor of God Church here in Detroit. I had the pleasure of leading her to the Lord shortly after I became born-again in the late 70s.

Shortly afterwards, Mama got a job and we moved into our own house. Even though George and I had only been dating a short time before my family moved to Chicago, I missed him. I'm not sure what I felt was love. I would guess it was more loneliness. I also missed my best friend, Bert. So, when they suggested coming to Chicago for a visit, I was excited. Once they got to Chicago, they decided that they wanted to move there. My mother agreed to let them stay in our home until they could find their own living quarters. That visit turned into a year's stay. Needless to say, space and beds were scarce and we all shared a bed with someone else. In my mother's absence, George and I also shared a bed.

I didn't want to marry George. I just wanted to leave home and shack up with him. But he refused, saying that he respected me too much to do that. He wanted to marry me but I was only 17 and needed Mama's legal permission to do so. She wouldn't give it. My primary reason for wanting to move in with George was to get away from Mama and all of her children. But also because Mama had started drinking and we couldn't stay in the same room together for more than 15 minutes without arguing. Family alienation was on the rise.

Mama was a quiet woman until she started drinking and then that "Party Girl" spirit she inherited from her Grandma Gertie emerged. She couldn't dance, but tried to. She couldn't drink either, but tried to. One or two drinks and she was stoned. The next day she would suffer greatly from a hangover, violently ill. When I asked, *"Mama, why do you do this?"* her reply was, *"It's our Indian blood."* Poor excuse, but with an element of truth. It was a generational pattern passed down to all of my mother's children, and eventually included me. I just had to get out of my mother's house. And I did.

Chapter 13

"Don't Do It!"

It really is as your mother tells you: marry too quickly, and you'll repent for the rest of your life.

From the very beginning, I knew that George and I shouldn't get married. We had absolutely nothing in common. A sure sign that we were making a mistake was when we got into a big argument just before our wedding day.

As soon as I turned 18 on October 11, 1960, we got a marriage license in Illinois, planning to use it in Michigan where most of our family and friends lived. Little did we know until we got back in Michigan a few days prior to the date we had set to be married that the Illinois license wasn't good in Michigan!

I will never forget the day we found out. We were in Downtown Detroit on Woodward Avenue. George blamed me and I blamed him for not knowing.

Disgusted with one another and panic-stricken, we each said, *"forget it,"* turned and walked away in the opposite direction. Ironically, a short time later, we both ended up at the same soda fountain at the old Woolworth Store on Woodward Avenue. In our ignorance, we took this as a "sign" that we should go ahead with the marriage.

Sometimes a "sign" is not what it seems to be. Besides, all of the invitations had been sent out and I had purchased my gown. Somehow we worked the marriage license situation out and were married in George's mother's home on October 29, 1960. I was 18; George was 22; and Darrell was five. Over the next 20 plus years, we lived to regret our decision a thousand times. My mother may not have had the best parenting skills, but she sure had intuition about that marriage.

Sadly, I can only remember one significant thing about my wedding day. My mother and her newest boyfriend got into a big fight during the reception. I was so embarrassed that I locked myself in one of the bedrooms and wouldn't come out for hours.

That night, my wedding night, I started my monthly cycle. Needless to say, George wasn't too happy about that!

After the wedding, we returned to Chicago to reside. Looking back, I wish that I could say that there were some good times in our marriage. If there were, I've had a memory lapse. Not only were there not any good times, there wasn't any love. If there was love, it certainly wasn't unconditional. We were both so young, so immature and so busy trying to get our own needs met.

Out of frustration, we each turned to someone else outside of our marriage. The man who came into my life was a Chicago police officer, a single father with two little girls. His name was Sam. We met in a meat market. I was 20. He was several years older. I can't recall now what attracted me to him, except to say that he was very kind and romantic. I needed to be noticed. By this time my marriage was falling apart and so was I.

After months of hiding and covering up my whereabouts with lies, I confessed my sin to George. He fell apart. First he hit the wall with his fist and then he hit me. It was the worst beating of my life. I can still hear his words echoing in my head, *"I'll never let you get close enough to hurt me again."*

Shortly afterwards, Sam informed me that he was going to move to California. He asked me to come. At first I refused. But things were getting worse and worse in my marriage to George. One day I quit my job, bought a train ticket, packed my son Darrell's clothes along with my own, and left George, moving to California to be with Sam. Darrell and I moved into his apartment with him and his two little girls. Darrell was seven and I was 20. Looking back, I can't help but wonder what Darrell thought about all of this. I don't remember him asking many questions.

My short time in California was disappointing. Sam had gotten a job as a private investigator and he expected me to take care of his two little girls while he worked. Suddenly, reality set in. It was as though I was back in my mother's house again taking care of her children. I wasn't ready to be a mother of three little children. Although I feel that the man I was with loved me, the feeling wasn't mutual. Almost as soon as I got there, I wanted to be back home. I called George and asked him to send for me. He did. Sam told me that I was making a big mistake and that George would *"make me pay for leaving him."* He was right. When I returned, things got even worse than they were before I left. In spite of the fact that I regretted what had happened, George never forgot it.

There came a point in time, however, when we decided to move back to Detroit. I believe we both hoped that things would be better for us. I came to Detroit first and found a lovely two-bedroom flat for $55.00 a month on the west side of Detroit. After paying $110.00 in Chicago for an apartment, this was unbelievable. Of course, that was in 1964. When I called and told George, he said *"Get Two!"* I quickly found a job at Chrysler Motor Car Company. Shortly thereafter, George came to Detroit and he also found a job there. It looked like things were getting better.

By this time, we had been married for four years. Both of us longed for a child. Darrell was nine years old, and he also wanted a brother. Although we tried hard to conceive, it didn't happen. Then, as is so often the case, while we were in the process of moving and the timing seemed so inappropriate: I got pregnant! After three months, I was threatening a miscarriage and had to quit my job. Neither of us cared about that. We were so happy about the pregnancy.

This might have been the only time in our marriage that I experienced any true happiness. But that didn't last long. George began to spend more and more time away from home. He said he was out gambling, but I had good reasons to doubt that. Sexual intimacy had stopped early in the pregnancy. I wanted it; he didn't. He said that he was *"afraid that he might hurt the baby."* I didn't believe him. In my heart, I knew that he was involved with another woman. I felt fat, ugly and rejected. It was a very depressing time.

Our son Donald was born on June 9, 1965 at Metropolitan Hospital in Detroit. At first they told us that we had a little girl. George was so happy. He had already picked out the name "Donna" for the "baby girl." Then they told us that we had twins! Finally, they got it right and brought me my beautiful baby boy. As soon as I looked at him, I knew he was mine. Looking back, Donald, his two children, Jason and Jasmyne, and my lovely mother-in-law Almeta Brooks, and George's sisters and brothers are the only good things that came out of this marriage. They have always loved and respected me. Thanks Fam!

After Donald was born, George continued staying away from home frequently, gambling. At least that's what he said. Six months later I went to work as a legal secretary at Osborne, Bell and Rice law firm in downtown Detroit. The office was located on the 24th floor of the Guardian Building. This is where I met my forever friend Shirley Reese, nee *"Couch."* We hit it off right away.

Shortly after meeting Shirley, she left the law firm and went to work at General Motors Corporation's headquarters on West Grand Boulevard. I followed her there in 1968 and stayed until 1976. We were among the first black women hired by General Motors. That was back in the days when we were given a Cost of Living Allowance (C.O.L.A.). The pay was so good that the employees called them "Generous Motors."

I like to tell the story about the day I went to General Motors to apply for a job. Just before I went there, I had gone down the street, on West Grand Boulevard, to Motown Records' main headquarters and applied for a job there. I was actually hired to work for Berry Gordy as a secretary. I was thrilled! However, I had the bright idea when leaving there that I should go down the street to General Motors and apply for a job there. In 1959 when I graduated from Northwestern High School, I had applied at GM for a job. At that time, they only had black elevator operators in the building. I was told to *"Come back in 10 years."* It wasn't quite 10 years, but I went back the same day that I was hired by Motown. I took the shorthand and typing test and went home. By the time I got home there was a message from GM's Personnel Department. I returned the call immediately and they offered me a job there as a secretary. When they told me the pay, I couldn't believe my ears. It was twice what I was offered by Motown. Of course, I accepted. After working for GM a short period of time, I was walking through the Personnel Department and stopped to speak to a young lady. To my amazement, she just happened to be the secretary that Motown had hired when I turned down the job. Motown was moving to Los Angeles and this young lady was out of a job. That could have been me.

One of the things that my forever friend Shirley and I had in common was the game *Scrabble*. On our lunch hour, we could eat lunch and play three games of *Scrabble* in one hour! And Shirley has always been a slow eater. I'm happy to say that after 40 years she and I are still the best of friends.... even though we don't get together much anymore for Scrabble.

Chapter 14

"Who is My Father?"

When it comes to your children, understand this: you can never go too far wrong telling them the truth right away, when they're little and can accept, process and receive it.

In spite of the fact that my marriage to George was still tumultuous, we bought our first home on Appoline Street. I'm grateful to my brother Steven for lending us some money to help with the down payment.

Darrell was 12 when we moved. It was seven years after George and I were married that he decided to legally adopt Darrell. Often I've thought back, trying to understand why it took so long. I don't have an answer. Because he was 12, that was considered the age of consent, and Darrell had to give permission to be adopted. We had never told him that he wasn't George's child. He didn't take that information well at all. And I made matters even worse. When he asked me

"Who is my father?" I said, *"It doesn't matter who your father was. George has raised you all of these years."*

Wrong answer. It did matter. It mattered a lot to him. Unfortunately, I couldn't tell him much about his father. I hardly knew him myself. This was a major turning point in Darrell's relationship with me. He despised me for keeping this secret from him. All I can say is that it's not easy being a mother, especially when you are 25 with a 12-year-old son. Years later I asked Darrell, on my knees, for his forgiveness. His penetrating words, *"I'll never forgive you,"* still pierce me today. He hasn't.

After being told about his birth, Darrell's behavior became totally unruly and uncontrollable. I spent many sleepless nights worrying about him. When he didn't come home, I didn't know whether to call the hospital, police station, or the morgue. He was skipping school and creating all kinds of havoc. He stayed in so much trouble when he did go that I think I went to school more than he did. I don't recall George ever going to school about either one of our sons. However, he was a very generous father and bought them many gifts. I recall once asking, *"Why doesn't Darrell ever come out of his room?"* It never dawned on us that he didn't have to. He had every material thing he needed right there in his room. At one point, he was even eating dinner in his room.

A parent should NEVER let their child eat dinner in his room.

The relationship between Darrell and George was fairly good until Donald came along. After all, Darrell had been through a lot: after he was told that George was not his father, and then George has a biological son. Naturally, George was more affectionate towards Donald than he was towards Darrell, and Darrell felt the difference as rejection.

To add to the trauma already going on at home, I made another bad decision.

Darrell had become interested in driving. George clearly told me not to let him drive my car. I didn't listen. One day Darrell asked if he could just back the car out of the driveway. I let him. Donald saw him driving, got excited, ran out of the house behind the car and got hit. George was at work. I left Darrell at home to explain what happened. Donald ended up in the emergency ward of the hospital. His leg had been broken, and he had to wear a full leg cast for many months. He spent his seventh birthday in a sling in the hospital. Looking back, I can see how devastating this had to be for Darrell, not only hitting his brother, but having to tell George.

One day Darrell and I had a huge argument. He cussed me out and I told him to get out of my house. He stormed out. I can still see the explosive anger on his face. He started running and never came back—except to ask me to sign papers for him to join the Navy. I did. He was 17 years old.

Chapter 15

New Beginnings

... Jesus declared. "Go now and leave your life of sin."
John 8:10 (NIV)

Darrell went off to the military and the pressure on my nervous system calmed somewhat. Eventually we moved from Appoline to Westwood. Although we changed our address, our marital problems moved along with us. There were many heated arguments and several instances of domestic violence. I was very lonely and started going with George to gamble. I wasn't good at gambling, so I started drinking. Like mother, like daughter. I couldn't drink much before I was drunk and acting like a fool. Afterwards, I would feel awful and embarrassed. More than once I can remember driving down Livernois Avenue in Detroit, in the section known historically as the "Avenue of Fashion," with one hand on the steering wheel and the other holding on to a glass of rum and Coke. I was blurry-eyed and driving in an out of traffic. It's a miracle that I ever made it home alive and without killing someone. One time this happened and George had to pick me up out of the car and carry me into our home. I recall him asking, *"Why do you do this? You know you can't drink!"* I remember either saying or thinking, *"Because I'm so unhappy."* Long ago, I had asked my mother that same question. Again, history was repeating itself.

Although my mother and I were both alcoholics, I was never a "party girl." When I got drunk, I usually just wanted to go to sleep. I guess that was my way of trying to escape the madness.

My attempts to escape were futile and I soon discovered that the only way to escape the madness was to physically leave it behind. On June 29, 1973, after 13 years of a miserable marriage, I divorced George in Wayne County Circuit Court. I was given the house on Westwood in the divorce settlement, along with custody of Donald.

For some reason, which is difficult for me to understand, I found it hard to be without George. I pursued him and we continued our physical relationship, in spite of the fact that I knew he was seeing someone else. Loneliness can make people do crazy things. As the saying goes, I was *"standing on stupid, looking for dumb."*

George had signed a lease on the apartment he moved

into for a year. Just before the lease was up, he asked if he could move back into my house. He promised that he would remarry me. I allowed him to do so. It didn't take long for me to realize that he had no intentions of keeping that promise. The arguments continued. His marital affairs became more obvious. When I confronted him about them, he didn't even deny it. In fact, his response was, *"I'll do what I want to do. We aren't married."*

In spite of George's extra-marital affairs, we remained together. However, in July 1976 I had a marvelous experience, a total life transformation.

My dear friend Shirley took Donald to a Christian camp. While at camp, Donald gave his heart to the Lord Jesus Christ. He was 10 years old. When he returned home, I noticed a big difference in him. He wasn't as rebellious as he had been in the past.

Donald brought home a Bible. He didn't read it, but I did. Although we were churchgoers at the time, we weren't into reading the Bible. I had no idea where to start, so I started with Genesis, which didn't make much sense to me at all. But I kept reading. When I mentioned this to Shirley, she told me to go to St. John and Romans. The lights came on! I began to see Jesus in a different way. Before, I saw Him as "someone up in heaven." But now I was beginning to see that He was Someone who wanted to come into my heart and live within me.

But the light was still dim. I was still struggling with my drinking problem, along with my marital challenges. But in 1976, God heard my groans and sent me a deliverer in the human form of Haman Cross, Jr., currently Pastor of Rosedale Park Baptist Church in Detroit.

Pastor Cross came to my church where I was a busy little church worker making pies and telling lies. How sad. I really believed that if I worked hard enough, God, in His mercy, would give me a break. I would escape hell, I hoped. Well, Pastor Cross came to teach a seminar on Evangelism. The little tool that he used was The Four Spiritual Laws, published by Campus Crusade for Christ. That handy little booklet will always be very special to me.

After going through the booklet with us, we were placed on a bus and driven out to Belle Isle Park in Detroit to share our faith. The first person I saw was a middle-aged Black man. I asked if he had a few minutes to talk to me. He was very accommodating. We sat down on the park bench and I began to go through The Four Spiritual Laws with him. When we got to the "Sinner's Prayer," for the first time I heard the Voice of God say to me:

"You haven't said this prayer yourself."

Of course, He was right. God is always right. I broke down and started crying, and the man on the bench next to me quickly took off. There I was trying to lead a soul to Christ without being saved myself! The soul turned out to ME! (I tell this story more fully in my book, The Fish Market.)

Although that was the happiest day of my life, things at home began to spiral down even more quickly. I left Springfield Baptist Church and joined Calvary Church of God in Christ. Pastor James E. Slappy insisted that we all be "Bible scholars." Today, I can truly say that my foundation in the Word was gained from my membership at Calvary.

I've been ordained or licensed on three different occasions by three different men of God: Bishop Jack Wallace of Detroit World Outreach; Pastor George Bogle, Founding Pastor (now retired) of Evangel Ministries in Detroit; and Pastor James E. Slappy. In 1977, Pastor James E. Slappy licensed me first as a missionary at Calvary COGIC.

Prior to that happening, one day I was leaving the church and the late Mother Lillian Sims, who was over the Women's Department, stopped and asked me *"Do you feel that God has a call on your life?"* I was startled. I didn't know what she meant by "a call." I thought to myself, *"Was my life here on earth over? Was God 'calling' me home to be with Him?"* I guess Mother Sims could tell by the puzzled look on my face that I was in a state of confusion. She hurriedly explained what a call meant. Her explanation consisted of her informing me that God had a plan and a purpose for my life to become an evangelist. Things became a little clearer to me at that point. Then Mother Sims asked me to bring the message to the church on the next Women's Day. Being a writer even back then, I had many journal messages already prepared. I didn't understand why until that very moment. I quickly responded, *"Yes, I will be happy to bring a message to the church."* My first message was from St. John 15:1-17. I particularly love verse 5:

"I am the vine; you are the branches. If a man remains in me and I in him, he will bear much fruit; apart from me you can do nothing."

Throughout my 25 years of full-time ministry, I have attempted to live by this passage and especially this verse.

George didn't appreciate my new life in Christ. He especially didn't like my new way of dressing. He expressed it very clearly one summer day, as I stood before him in the blistering sun wearing a long-sleeved sundress with a turtleneck tee shirt underneath it, thick stockings, loafers, hair combed back in a bun and no lipstick! George looked at me and said these words, *"It looks like you go out of your way to be ugly."* Needless to say, I felt offended, rejected, and unappreciated!

I've changed my look since then, and my understanding of what "sanctified" means. But I can imagine how I must have looked to him. A sanctified M-E-S-S!

Chapter 16

Flipping the Script

"Therefore if any man be in Christ,
he is a new creature; old things are passed away;
behold, all things are become new."
2 Cor. 5:17

Although I was troubled by my living arrangements with George before my transformation experience, I became even more convicted when I became born again. In my heart, I knew that I was living in sin and had been for seven years. I wanted out. I asked George to leave over and over again, but he refused. The decision was left up to me. It was 1981.

The night before I left I told George that I was going to leave in the morning. That night I laid on the sofa in the living room and prayed that George would come out of the bedroom and ask me to stay. He didn't. Finally, the Lord gave me peace. This is what He told me: *"I have given you a new husband. You are now the Bride of Christ. Come out from among them and be ye separated"*(Isa. 54:5; 2 Cor. 6:17).

By this time, I had already left General Motors and I had no employment. I wasn't sure how I was going to make it, but I packed up my things, and the next morning I took my child and left. Darrell was already in the Navy. I thought, *"If my mother could do it with five children and no place to go, surely I could do it."* The only regret that I have is that I allowed him to come back into the house in the first place. As a result of that poor decision, I lost my house which had been given to me in the divorce settlement. But, praise be to God, I've had two better homes since then. But really, I have the one thing that cannot be bought: peace of mind.

When George continued to be adamant about leaving, there was only one thing for me to do: after 20 years of pure hell, I left. I moved into the home of my dear friend Carolyn Thomas. Carolyn was a single working mother, but she took me in. Donald went to live with my sister Sharon and her family.

With George out of my life, I wanted a completely new start. Not only did I leave George, but I also left my church, where I was a licensed missionary. I'm sure that some of them knew that George and I weren't married. I felt it best to move on.

I was an emotional wreck when I moved in with Carolyn. I cried day and night. I tried to work through a temporary agency, but couldn't get through the day without breaking down in tears. I had to leave the job. I tried to help keep the house clean, but getting out of bed was a major challenge. I could barely keep myself clean. Although Carolyn was kind enough to allow me to stay in one of her bedrooms, I slept on the floor day and night. I could have mopped the floor with my tears.

December 31, 1981: New Years Eve at Carolyn's house. She was getting ready to go to church for Watch Night Service. *"Come on and go with me,"* she urged. I had crawled up under the coffee table and wouldn't come out. Indeed, I was having my own "Auld Lang Syne" experience and "old acquaintances needed to be forgotten." Carolyn left for Watch Night, The pain and rejection I was feeling from my relationship with George and his many open affairs were working their way through my very body, it seemed, and I was breaking down. I don't remember midnight or when the tears stopped flowing.

Looking back, I do believe that I had a nervous breakdown – and didn't know it! God kept me through it all – And then He rewarded me for doing the right thing.

Chapter 17

Breaking the Ties that Bind

Never, under any circumstances, let any human being drive you mad. Before you do that, leave.

As I said earlier, this has not been an easy book to write. The chapter you are about to read is the most difficult. In fact, it was so hard that I started to leave it out. But I feel that I must include it for my children's sake, as well as to help those who may be reading this book. This chapter is written to all of you women and young girls who allow men to get into your mind and drive you crazy. So, since I've already spilled so much of my guts, I might as well spill the rest.

On more than one occasion, I've heard on the news or read in the newspapers where a wife or woman has murdered her man and gone to prison for the rest of her life. I can't help but wonder if any of them sitting in a prison cell right now went in there born again. But, for the grace of God, one of those women could have been me. During my miserable 20-year marriage (the last seven of them common-law) to George Brooks, I attempted to kill him three times! Not only was I saved and speaking in tongues, but I was a licensed minister of the gospel of Jesus Christ. Yet I snapped. Not once; not twice; but three times.

Although I'm not sure that I loved George when we got married, somewhere along the way I fell madly in love with him. I emphasize the word "madly" because that's exactly what it was. The root word for madly is "mad." Webster's Dictionary describes "mad" as "disordered in mind; insane; being rash and foolish; I was all of these. While I was standing on stupid looking for dumb, George was having one open affair after another. It appeared to me that he didn't even try hard to hide it. Many people knew. In the midst of this, I was slowly losing my mind.

The first time I attempted to kill him was after he had been out all night. I knew that there was a gun somewhere in our home. In a state of rage, I tore up our home looking for the gun. By the time he came home the house was in shambles. Thank God that I didn't find the gun.

The second time I attempted to kill him was with a car. We had one of our many arguments. I ran out of the house, jumped in the car, and sped out of the driveway. George had run out the side door behind me. I saw him but didn't brake. The car missed him by inches. Had he not jumped back just in time, he would have been flattened out in the driveway and the police would have been putting handcuffs on me and hauling my miserable behind to jail. Thank God for giving George quick reflexes.

The last time I attempted to kill him was when I found him in my home with another woman. By this time we had separated. But, you may recall that I had been given the house in our divorce settlement earlier. So I still perceived it as my house, even though he had forced me to move out by his refusal to leave himself.

This particular day I had gone by the house to visit my son Donald who had moved back home with his father. The mistake I made was not calling first.

When I arrived at the house, the lock had been changed, and George wouldn't answer the doorbell. There was evidence that he was there because there were two cars in the driveway – his and another. The house had a large picture window, which I looked through as I continued to furiously ring the doorbell and bang on the door, yelling and screaming to the top of my lungs, *"Let me in! Let me in!"* Looking through the window, I saw a naked woman run from the bedroom into the bathroom. I became enraged. I know from personal experience that there is a fine line between sanity and insanity.

It was trash day on the street and the garbage was at the curb. My insanity told me to dump the trash and set it

AND the house on fire. I got as far as dumping the trash, but had no matches, and the cigarette lighter in the car didn't work. At this point, I jumped in my car and took off for the corner store to get some matches.

I can still recall my anxiousness as I stood in the line trying to quickly get waited on to buy matches to set the house on fire. I hopped from one foot to the other and sweat was pouring off my brow. (Or maybe it was tears; I don't remember now.) Finally, I got to the front of the line, got the matches, and rushed out of the store. Thank God for the slow line. When I returned George and the woman were gone. I got back in my car and broke down. I believe that I sat there and cried a river of tears. All I could think about is that I had given 20 years of my life to a man who had continuously humiliated and rejected me. Finally, I regained my composure enough to drive away.

Even though George was physically out of my life, emotionally and spiritually there was a soul tie there. My mind was being held captive. After seeing what I saw through the window, that image was implanted in my mind. When I went to bed at night, I dreamed that I was in bed with another woman. *"What is this?"* I asked myself. *"Why am I laying beside another woman and embracing her? I'm not a lesbian."* Night after night I had that same dream of being in bed with a woman. *"Oh, God, help me,"* I cried out to the Lord. *"Give me understanding."* And He did. This is what he showed me...

Any complete sexual act, whether fornication, adultery, or homosexuality, unites a person's soul with the other. *"Or do you not know that the one who joins himself to a harlot (or any other illicit partner) is one body with her? For He says, "The two will become one flesh"* (1 Cor. 6:16). Thus, whatever woman a man enters, their souls are united to each other from that moment on. Simply put, because George and I were united in (holy) matrimony to each other, our spirits became one. Thus, when that bond was violated, every sexual relationship we ever had outside of that marriage was brought into our union. The Bible says that what God has joined together, let no man put asunder. Looking at this revelation, it's easy for me to see why God banned divorce and that fornication, adultery and homosexuality are sins in the eyes of God. I pray that those who are reading this will take heed to God's word and depart from evil, and that the captives will be set free.

Mistakes made early in life impact the rest of our lives. Some become involved sexually without the commitment of marriage. Maybe you believed him when he told you that he loved you. Perhaps you really did think that yielding would show your true love, and that if you didn't yield you would lose that person. I made that mistake at a very early age. Or, maybe you simply wanted to have a good time without thinking about the consequences. I'm here to tell you that there are consequences. As I look at my family: my children and grandchildren, and now my great grandchildren, I can see how fleshly decisions made by the parents have had a negative impact on all of them.

Finally, let me say this: If we don't deal with what's happened in the family tree, and if we don't deal with what's in our personal lives, our children will inherit our curses. So, dear friend, I encourage you to go before the Lord and get your life straightened out so that you can break the power of sin, so that genetically inherited diseases no longer exist. Sin is a disease, just like cancer.

What To Do If You Feel You Have Generational Issues That Need To Be Broken—

Ask the Lord to reveal any generational curse or sin issue.

Ask the Lord how many generations back in the family line this generational curse was first empowered.

Ask the Lord what happened to empower that event.

Renounce, repent, and ask forgiveness for any sin committed in the family line. This is called "identification repentance."

Ask the Lord Jesus to cover the family line and the memory or incident with His blood. Renounce and repent for sin related to that event.

Ask the Lord to break all ungodly connections from that event in the generational line to the present.

Demand all evil to go wherever Jesus commands them.

End the session with prayer for the cleansing and protection of the Holy Spirit.

Chapter 18

Mr. Wright or Mr. Wrong

Sanctification—moving toward holiness—is a process. Remember that, and submit to the process as you listen to God's voice.

Even though my mother had many bad relationships with men, including three failed marriages, and even though I had a devastating marriage with George, I always felt that God wanted me to have a happy, successful marriage. And I always wanted to be married. Perhaps that's why I stayed with George as long as I did. More than once someone would ask me, *"Are you a pastor's wife?"* These were words of encouragement to me in the midst of my distress. I couldn't help but think that one day George would be saved and become a pastor and I would become a pastor's wife. Of course, that never happened. What people were seeing is the man that was about to come into my life.

In spite of my well-meaning friends who told me, *"Girl, there's a male shortage out here. Don't get your hopes up too high,"* I believed that God had just the right man for me. My response to them was, *"Hey, there may be a male shortage, but there's no tree shortage. If He has to, God will take a tree and make me a man!"* I knew what I was looking for and had a shopping list close by for reference. If an imposter came along, I would surely recognize him. And one did.

It was the first Christmas Eve after George and I had gone our separate ways. I was in the drugstore trying to buy a Christmas card. I say "trying to buy" because nothing seemed appropriate. They all said, "Merry Christmas," and it certainly wasn't a Merry Christmas for me. Holiday time can be a very difficult time when you're alone. And I was alone.

Suddenly, Mr. Wright came up alongside of me. I can't remember his exact words, but he was obviously making a pass at me. The next thing I knew he was inviting me to go to the show with him. Of course, I refused. My common sense said no, but I was so lonely that a part of me wanted to say yes. However, I did give him my phone number and he called. Eventually, I agreed to go out with him. Mr. Wright was quite a gentleman, handsome, fun, and very complimentary, which is something that I certainly needed at the time, having experienced so much rejection.

Although this fine man had everything on my list that I was looking for, one very important thing was missing: he wasn't saved. And he made it clear that he wasn't interested in changing his ways. He was also quite disturbed when I told him that we would have to have a platonic relationship. Even though he didn't verbally say it, his facial expression was loud and clear. *"NO SEX? You've got to be kidding!"* But I wasn't. I had said "Yes" too many times before when I should have said "No." Nevertheless, we continued the relationship and I held fast to my word: *"No Sex."*

One day Jim said to me, *"Okay. If you want a platonic relationship, I'll go along with that. But, if you call me one weekend and don't get an answer, don't ask me where I've been."* That was obviously a threat. But I didn't yield. One weekend, however, that did happen. I called him and he wasn't home - gone all weekend. His words echoed in my ears. I knew that I couldn't ask him where he had been. Reality set in. That was the end of our relationship. I cut him loose. Mr. Wright was Mr. Wrong.

But Mr. Right was getting closer and closer.

When I left George and moved in with Carolyn, I took a few pieces of furniture that belonged to me personally. I put those pieces in storage.

After living with Carolyn for a few months, I began to get a handle on my emotions and feel better. But I still didn't have a job or any money and I owed some bills. This was troubling me.

One day I sat on the side of the bed and I heard the Voice of God say, *"Add up your bills."* When I did, they totaled about $1,000. Within a few days, George sent me exactly $1,000 from an old insurance policy on me that he had cashed in. To God be the glory! This gave me a lot of relief, enough where I was able to go out and get a job as an office manager at the American Red Cross on Mack Avenue in Detroit. It didn't pay the salary that I had been accustomed to getting at General Motors. But God spoke to my heart and told me that He had sent me there to minister to my supervisor who was lonely and really needed a friend. Clara was a very smart woman, a Red Cross administrator not much older than I. She had very little social life because she cared for her aged mother. Clara and I became friends. I introduced her to Mr. Wright, and they ironically began dating.

Shortly after getting the job at the Red Cross, I rented an apartment at Alden Park Towers, an old prestigious building on Jefferson Avenue in Downtown Detroit. It was a large, two bedroom apartment. I had gotten two bedrooms because I thought that Donald was going to come and live with me. By this time, he had left my sister Sharon's home and gone back to live with his father. Prior to our leaving George, Donald had attended Calvary Church Of God In Christ regularly. After the separation, he stopped going to church. I regret that Donald couldn't stay with me; there just wasn't room at Carolyn's house. His going to Sharon's home was supposed to be a temporary arrangement until I could find adequate housing for us both. At the time, Donald was 17 and had dropped out of high school.

Was I abandoning him by sending him to live with my sister? I didn't think so. I was simply doing the best I could to make a better life.

Oh, if we could only see in advance how bad marriages affect our children, we might be more careful about going into this institution!

Chapter 19

God Has Smiled on Me

The boundary lines have fallen for me in pleasant places; surely I have a delightful inheritance.
Ps. 16:16 (NIV)

It was in May 1982 that I moved alone into Alden Park Towers. Donald had returned to his father's home and Darrell was in the Navy. One morning, as I was getting ready for work, I was singing one of my favorite songs, *"God Has Smiled On Me."* I continued singing, as I walked to the parking lot to get in my car. When I got to the spot where I had left the car – IT WAS GONE! Strangely enough, I continued singing. I even broke out in joyful laughter. This was even more strange. I recall saying out loud, *"Now, I know that I left my car here."* But it was gone. Shaking my head, I slowly walked back inside to my apartment, called my job to let them know what had happened. Then I called the police to report the car stolen. Later I took the bus to work. I seemed to have a perfect peace about the whole thing. It didn't take me long to discover why.

My move to Alden Park Towers had been frightening to me. I was nearly 40 years old and had never lived alone. Although I had a large apartment, I slept on the floor by the front door in case someone tried to break into the apartment they would fall over me first!

Because of my fear of living alone, when I returned from my job each evening I would go to the community room and stay there as long as I could. I became quite sociable. In my mind, going there was my survival tactic.

This was a very lonely time for me. I was sure that my friends would come to visit since I had this beautiful apartment on the Detroit River. But they didn't come. My mother lived in Windsor, right across the bridge from Detroit. She didn't come either. No one came. It was as though God had lifted me up from where I was and put me in a totally new environment. Soon I found out why.

After work one day, I took a short cut to my apartment through the parking lot. There I saw a black Concord with a sticker on the rear bumper. The sticker said, "Joy of Jesus." I recall thinking, *"Someone here knows the Lord."* I wanted to know who it was, so I pulled out a piece of paper, the only thing I had was a gospel tract, and wrote a note saying, *"I love your bumper sticker. Please give me a call."* Little did I know who it would be. It could have been a visitor in the apartment building, a little old lady, a married man. It could have been anyone. But it turned out to be Rev. Eddie K. Edwards, founder of Joy of Jesus Ministries on the east side of Detroit! He had lived in the building for 12 years. He hardly knew anyone there. This had been his place of refuge. On the other hand, I probably knew most of the residents the first month I lived there.

Eddie did call and that's when I discovered that "Joy of Jesus" was a ministry. We must have talked on the phone for over an hour. The organization ministered to children through a summer camping program in Kingston, Michigan. I was really impressed to learn that every summer 600 kids went to the Joy of Jesus summer camp. I was also impressed when he slipped a Joy of Jesus newsletter under my door. I was even more impressed when I couldn't find any errors in the publication! Being a writer, and having been a proofreader at General Motors for many years, I was accustomed to critiquing written materials. I wanted to know more about this organization...and the man!

Eddie called to see if I had received and read the materials. I told him that I had and that I was impressed. He invited me to have dinner with him. It was a Tuesday and we went to Big Boy's restaurant on Jefferson Avenue across from Belle Isle.

When we went out to dinner, I noticed that he didn't order. *"Aren't you hungry?"* I asked. *"I always fast on Tuesdays,"* was his reply. He told me that his life's scripture was Isaiah 58:12:

"And they that shall be of thee shall build the old waste places; thou shalt raise up the foundations of many generations; and thou shall be called the repairer of the breach. The restorer of paths to dwell in."

This scripture speaks about God's chosen fast. I couldn't understand why he didn't choose another day of the week to invite me to dinner.

Thinking back, I have to laugh. He probably couldn't afford to feed himself and me too! Eddie was so broke. He had quit a high level job in corporate America at AT&T to start Joy of Jesus Ministries. Over the years, I watched him make many personal sacrifices. While we were at dinner, I gave him my resume. I believe he was as impressed by my resume as I was with his newsletter.

I must say that I fell in love with Eddie at first sight. The day he came to my door to pick me up for dinner I heard the Voice of the Lord say, *"This is your husband."* God was right. Of course, God is always right. By the way, I got my car back.

Shortly after Eddie started driving me to work and to his church, Bethesda, formerly pastored by James E. Beall, I received a phone call from the Detroit Police Department. They informed me that they had my car at their headquarters on Gratiot near Conner. Eddie took me to the station. We saw my car in the parking lot as soon as we entered the premises. When I told the Captain at the desk why I was there he said,

"Lady, we don't bring cars in here when they are stolen. We call and tell you which towing company to pick them up from."

"But, sir," I said, *"My car is sitting right outside in your parking lot."* His response surprised both Eddie and I, *"Well, get it and go."* And that's exactly what we did. The only thing wrong with the car was that the battery was missing! Eddie got another one, put it in and we left. To this day, we don't understand how that car got to the police station.

I moved into Alden Park Towers in May. I met Eddie in June. He proposed in July. It wasn't a very romantic proposal. No billboard. No engagement party. No bended knee. No engagement ring. The way it happened was on the telephone! We were having a conversation. This is the way it went:

EDDIE: "Do you plan to get married again some day?"
MARY: "Yes."
EDDIE: "How will you know when you are ready?"
MARY: "I have a written list of what I'm looking for in a man."
EDDIE: "Oh? And what's on that list?"
MARY: "A man like you."
EDDIE: (Laughingly said) "Then why don't you marry me?"
MARY: (Stunned, I replied) "Why don't you ask?"
EDDIE: "Will you marry me?"
MARY: (In a state of joyful glee) 'YES!"

We were married on Sweetest Day, October 16, 1982, at my home church, Calvary Church Of God In Christ, by the late Pastor James E. Slappy. His lovely wife Claudette Slappy was my matron of honor. She and I are friends to this day. Unfortunately, we are both widows now. Pastor Slappy passed in March 2005.

Eddie and I had a morning wedding at Calvary. They had just moved into their new building and had forgotten to turn on the heat. It was so cold that I had to marry in my gown and fur stole. Our guests were shivering, but Eddie and I were warm!

Earlier I mentioned to you that I had a shopping list of what I was looking for in a husband. God gave me everything on the list that I desired – and more. He did exceedingly, abundantly, above all that I could ask or even think. I read from my list at our wedding:

- *A man who is saved and spirit filled*
- *A man who will love me as Christ loves the church*
- *A man who loves to read, and especially the Bible*
- *A "ministry-minded" man*
- *A "family-minded" man*
- *A man who is self-motivated and will motivate me*
- *A man who understands and appreciates my gifts/ talents*
- *A man who is kind and patient*
- *A man who loves children and seniors*
- *A man who has good hygiene and a sharp dresser*
- *A man who is sociable and hospitable*

- *A man who is generous and a cheerful giver*
- *A man who loves peanuts and popcorn*
- *A man who is easy to feed*
- *A man who likes to travel*

Mr. Wright and Clara attended the wedding. The two of them were so happy for me. I can't recall what Clara gave me for a wedding present. But 'Mr. Wright' gave me a little soap dish! Even that is symbolic; I washed my hands of him and God kept me clean!

Occasionally, when people would ask Eddie how we met, he would jokingly say, *"She picked me up."* Then he would tell the story about me leaving a note on his car. Sometimes I would be embarrassed. But, one day, I prayed about it and God gave me just what to say. The next time Eddie made that statement, I laughed and said, *"That's right. And I took him to a whole new level!"* I never heard him say that again.

Mary's grandmother (left), mother, (center) and unidentified relative.

Mary and her mother on her 50th birthday.

Mary's mother, (right) assisting as nurse during baptism at church.

Mary and Eddie on her 60th birthday.

Mary (seated, left center) with Eddie, staff and kids at Joy of Jesus.

Mary (r) with Dr. J. Victor and Min. Catherine B. Eagan.

Chapter 20

Moving to Ravendale

Also, seek the peace and prosperity of the city to which I have carried you into exile. Pray to the Lord for it, because if it prospers, you too will prosper."
Jer. 29:7

Due to a lack of finances, our honeymoon was a weekend stay at the Hyatt-Regency in Dearborn, Michigan. We had sold some of our belongings and packed others, preparing to move to a rented house on the west side of Detroit. However, while we were away, the owner of the home had a major crisis. She was engaged to be married, and her fiancé broke off the engagement. She was absolutely devastated, and so were we. Our notice to move had been given to Alden Park Towers and we had nowhere to go. She didn't know how to break the horrible news to us. When we went to her home to speak to her, understandably, she was an emotional wreck. God used Eddie and me to minister to her. He used us to bring peace in the midst of a terrible storm. Eddie remembers this as being one of the major highlights in our marriage. So do I.

When you go through life, you spread blessings wherever there is opportunity and you never know when God is going to return your blessings back to you but rest assured, He will. As it turned out, God intervened in our housing situation and we were able to retain our apartment at Alden Park Towers. We had both given up our leases, but they allowed us to remain in the one I had.

I had two jobs when I married Eddie. One was full time at The American Red Cross and the other a part time job selling jewelry. Because I made more money on my part time job than on my full time job, I quit The Red Cross and began working full time at Joy of Jesus as a volunteer. Shortly after that, I also quit the part time job to spend more time in the ministry, still working as a volunteer.

When we got married in 1982, Joy of Jesus was six years old. They were in a storefront on Outer Drive and Conant. There was one large working area, Eddie's private office, and a unisex restroom. At that time, all the ministry had was the summer camp program and a once-a-week after school program called "Care Units." Volunteers would pick up the children and take them to various churches that were kind enough to allow us to use their buildings...for a while, anyway. But before long the deacons began to complain about outside children using their churches and we knew that we needed to have our own headquarters for the children.

About this time, the Lord directed us to go to Word of Life Camp in Schroon Lake, New York, founded by Jack Wyrtzen. We were introduced to this family camp by my former Pastor James E. Slappy at Calvary Church Of God In Christ. Every summer Calvary would take the youth department to this lovely camp. Before I met Eddie, my son Donald was one of the youths who went. This is where Donald gave his heart to the Lord. He was only 10 years old at the time. Interestingly, Donald and Eddie both gave their hearts to Jesus at a summer camp when they were about the same age. The summer camp experience for Eddie later became his motivation for starting Joy of Jesus Ministries. Personally, I never attended a camp as a child. We fell in love with this beautiful place. This was a divine connection; the presence of the Lord was all around. Such a serene setting with rolling hills, stately trees, and beautiful lakes. One of the things we really appreciated about the camp is that it had a family atmosphere, with activities for parents and children alike.

Towards the end of the week, the entire family came together for fellowship. We could see the importance of the family vacationing together and yet having time for themselves. It was everything we wanted in a family camp. We sat on a hilltop and prayed to the Lord to bless us according to what our eyes beheld. *"Help us find something in Michigan like this,"* we asked Him together.

We knew exactly what we wanted in a camp, but we

also knew that we wanted to be in a specific neighborhood full of children. We needed the beauty of Schroon Lake in the heart of the city of Detroit. Where would we find it?

When we returned home from Word of Life Camp, Eddie contacted a real estate agent who handled property for the Archdiocese of Detroit. We told him that we wanted to be in a neighborhood where there were lots and lots of children. We also gave him a detailed description of want we wanted. Then we told him that we didn't have any money! The agent looked at us incredulously and said, *"Well, I know the exact building you have described. It's the former St. Ignatius Grade School building on the east side of Detroit on Camden Street. But it's for sale for $180,000!"*

At that time, we were still in the storefront, where we were barely able to pay the monthly rent of $250. When Eddie told the agent that we wanted to see the building, I couldn't believe my ears. *"Surely, I've married a crazy man,"* I thought to myself. To be honest with you, I really didn't understand my husband's level of faith back then. My philosophy, learned at childhood, was never buy anything you can't afford. So, when he suggested that we look at the building, I was hoping that was all we were going to do.

The building was located in the Ravendale Community on Camden Street near City Airport. It was an immaculate 17,000 square feet building, with two floors. The hallway was a block long. We could have set the storefront where we were presently located into that building four times—with room to spare! It even had two restrooms on the first floor—no more unisex restroom! There were many classrooms and an administrative office in the front of the building. It had a huge gymnasium and a commercial kitchen. Upstairs there were more offices. Looking at the upstairs, my mind began to see an *"Upper Room,"* such as that described in the Book of Acts. *"How wonderful,"* I thought to myself. *"We can have a chapel and prayer room up here."* Yes! Visions of an *"Upper Room"* experience began to dance in my head. Although it wasn't the scenic atmosphere we had experienced at Word of Life Camp in Schroon Lake, there were modest little houses on the block, flower pots on the porches, and patches of grass here and there. We could see potential.

As we continued to walk through the building, I knew that Eddie had to have it; God was starting to deal with me as well, especially with regard to the "Upper Room," which later did become our prayer room. I named it "The Master's Pasture." Weekly Bible Studies were held there for staff and community.

After looking at the building, Eddie said, *"We are going to bring our board of directors through here and see what they have to say. We will take a vote and, if one person votes 'no,' then that will be the end of it."* Well, I was sure that was going to be the end of our amusement. We had a very conservative board.

How wrong I was! They went through the building

and took a vote. Everyone said, *"Yes, let's go for it,"* except one person who abstained. Eddie took that as a clear *"yes."*

The building was owned by The Archdiocese of Detroit and was being rented to Northeast Guidance Center who had lost some government funding and had to move out. It was boarded up and being used in the evenings by the Police Athletic League (P.A.L.). The Northeast Guidance Center was anxious to get out of the lease and The Archdiocese was anxious to sell the building. We were anxious to buy it. We told the agent that we wanted to purchase the building and from that point on God performed miracle after miracle. Since we didn't have any money, The Archdiocese was willing to give us a $30,000 balloon down payment. We had to put up $1,000 as a good faith gesture. Where did we get the $1,000 from? I have no idea.

It was winter, and just as the purchase agreement was about to be signed between Joy of Jesus and The Archdiocese, some kids got into the boiler room and turned off the pipes. There was a huge flood throughout the building, destroying the floor in the block-long hallway and the carpet in all of the classrooms. It was a disaster. Joy of Jesus was about to back out of the deal. We certainly didn't have any money to renovate. But God intervened on our behalf. The Archdiocese was heavily covered with insurance. They promised that if we went through with the deal that they would give us all of the insurance money to renovate the building. We bought the deal, and they kept their promise. We moved in and renovated the building with a few paid maintenance people, but mostly volunteers. Indeed, the Lord blessed.

When our lease was up at Alden Park Towers, we bought our first home. It was on Corbett Street in the Ravendale Community. We bought a lovely, well-kept, brick bungalow, and the mortgage payment was much cheaper than our rent at Alden Park Towers. We were often teased that we lived in the "suburbs" of Ravendale. Our home was on the outskirts of the 36-block area that we had carved out for our community revitalization work. In fact, we had to open up the boundaries to include our home. Eddie promised that we would only be there for five years. Ten years later we moved out.

Obviously it was the Lord's will for Joy of Jesus and the Edwardses to move to Ravendale. The BIG question was, how were we going to pay for the building? For that matter, how were we even going to pay our own mortgage? We had no government dollars and no guaranteed funding. If the money didn't come in, Eddie didn't get paid. This was surely going to take an Act of God.

MEMORIES…

HE MAKES ALL THINGS NEW

© 1993 Mary Edwards

When Eddie and I moved to Ravendale
All we could see were houses for sale
Frightened residents had begun to flee
Looking for a safer community
Abandoned houses were an awful sight
Hardly a place you wanted to be at night
Unscrupulous folks moving in
Turned the houses into crack dens

Children were skipping school
Nowhere to go and nothing to do

Fragile families were falling apart
What they needed was a new start

Using the anointed Joy of Jesus Staff
God gave the people a life raft

When Jesus comes to the rescue
Behold, He makes all things new

NEIGHBORHOOD NOISES

In my neighborhood, it's hard to sleep
Radios blast and car horns beep

Cats meow and dogs growl
Burglars are on the prowl

Airplanes flying overhead
Cause us to toss and turn in bed

Husbands and wives yell at each other
Angry neighbors shout, "Shut up, brother"

Doors slam and glass breaks
Frightened neighbors tremble and shake

Shrilling siren sounds keep us awake
We want to cry, "Give us a break."

But instead we close the windows tight
Then we suffer another hot, sweaty night.

Chapter 21

A Neighborhood Redeemed

Trust in the LORD, and do good; dwell in the land and cultivate faithfulness.
Ps. 37:3 NAS

Pastor James E. Beall of Bethesda Church, my husband's mentor for many years, came to dedicate the building in the spring of 1984. Eddie told all of us, *"Brother Jim has a very high standard of excellence. I want us to have this building spotless when he comes."* I wouldn't be a bit surprised if one of our maintenance men "spit-polished" the floor in that block-long hallway. The new floor shined like the noonday sun. Eddie beamed when he did the inspection prior to Pastor Jim's arrival. Pastor Jim was well pleased.

When we moved into our headquarters, we had very little furniture but many rooms that were going to eventually be used for offices, as well as classrooms for the children.

Prophetic words came daily that *"God is going to give you so much furniture that you will have an abundance to share with the needy."* And we did. On a regular basis, trucks from major corporations throughout the city were pulling up and dropping off desks, chairs, file cabinets, and typewriters, thanks to the efforts of our diligent board of directors who appealed to their friends, associates, and employers. Indeed, we had an abundance to share with churches and other non-profit organizations such as ourselves.

Oh, happy day! Except how were we going to pay the $1,900 monthly mortgage on the building, and the $30,000 balloon payment in a year? That's what kept troubling me. I soon found out. God had a ram in the bush: me!

One day Eddie was invited to go to a fundraising seminar. He couldn't go, so he sent me. Little did I know what I was getting into. At the seminar, the speaker introduced himself and then asked us to introduce ourselves. Immediately, I found favor with the presenter. He was teaching about how to have a "Faith Commitment Banquet," and continuously used Joy of Jesus as an example. He made it seem so easy and I was excited enough to go back and tell Eddie, *"I think we can do this."* Eddie always liked people who took initiative. He was pleased with my optimism and said, *"Let's call the gentleman up and have him come and tell us more the next time he's in town."* I called him, and a few days later he called to say that he had been invited by someone else to return to Detroit and that he would call us when he arrived.

When he returned, he came to Joy of Jesus. I was called into Eddie's office after he had been meeting with the man for a couple of hours. The two of them had agreed that we needed to start a Development Department, a nice name for fundraising. They had also agreed that I was the one who should direct it. Before I knew it, I had been drafted. I was put in a position where I couldn't refuse. I also knew that if we didn't do something quick, we would be behind in our mortgage and also wouldn't have the $30,000 balloon payment that we had originally agreed to.

At this point, I began to multi-task. I was still the volunteer coordinator. But now I had taken on the task of development director, spiritual director for the staff, and community Bible study teacher. And, of course, I was still Eddie's wife and we had evening social and ministerial responsibilities. I was really beginning to feel overwhelmed.

Prior to my new assignment as development director, I was the volunteer coordinator. But even though I didn't get paid, I loved my work. It seemed so natural for me to get people to help us. I liked people and they liked me.

One of the amazing things that I was able to do was to coalesce volunteers to canvass the neighborhood with a 52-question needs assessment that Eddie had me develop. The amazing part is that many of the volunteers were suburbanites and they were going door-to-door asking the residents to fill out these questionnaires – WHILE THEY WAITED IN

THEIR HOMES. Ravendale was a drug-infested, high crime neighborhood. These volunteers were some very courageous people. God bless them even now. Bob and Theresa Zabick were major supporters and canvassers.

I have a confession to make here. When Eddie asked me to craft the 52-question survey, I didn't know where to begin. I had never done anything like that before. And, in spite of me asking him repeatedly to help me, he wouldn't. All he said is, *"Just do the best you can."* I was furious. It was one of the hardest things I ever had to do in the ministry. Little did I know at the time that one day that same questionnaire would be used across the country in organizations doing neighborhood development.

The feedback from those surveys helped us establish the Ravendale Community Revitalization Project. For more information about this survey, email me at: ministermaryedwards@yahoo.com.

I was the spiritual development director for the ministry and community Bible study teacher. In addition, I wrote the grant that prompted United Community Services to give us $100,000 to start our family life center, Camden House.

Chapter 22

From Camden House to the White House

Unless the Lord builds the house, they labor in vain that build it...
Ps. 127:1

When we moved into Ravendale, we originally thought it was for the children only. It didn't take us long to see that the entire family needed to be included.

This revelation came to us the day that one of the neighborhood residents came to Joy of Jesus looking for clothing. She was inebriated and became unruly. I was called into the storage room where she and the clothing were. After I calmed her down, she told me that it really wasn't the clothing that she came for. She admitted that she and her husband were both alcoholics and that she was concerned about the future of her children. I began to minister to her and assure her that Jesus could help her and her family. We prayed and before my very eyes she began to sober up. I literally saw hope emerge in her face. After selecting some clothing, she prepared to leave. I promised to get back with her.

That evening I went to Eddie and shared the story with him. He was all ears. The next day I gathered together some of the ladies from the community Bible study group. In a round table discussion, I asked them to describe their needs. From that data, I developed the vision for the New Start in Life Program. It was in 1984. The vision sat in the file for six years. We didn't have the money to fully implement the program. But in the meantime, we did the best we could to keep hope alive among the families. In essence, I had taken on another role: serving as the Family Life Director. I was still multi-tasking, but I longed to be free to serve solely as the Family Life Director for the New Start in Life Program. God heard my cry.

"Write the vision. Though it tarry, it shall come to pass" (Hab. 2:2)

It was in 1990, as Eddie was serving on the United Community Services Crime Task Force, when the group began talking about getting families involved in fighting crime in the neighborhood As he listened, Eddie realized that what they needed was the vision that I had written and filed away in 1984—six years earlier. He presented it at the table and they encouraged him to write up the request for money. We developed a *"Family Approach to Crime and Treatment"* (F.A.C.T.)

proposal to work with ten families in the Ravendale Community for one year, teaching them life coping skills. We asked for $50,000.

Joy of Jesus was one of ten organizations to receive the F.A.C.T. grant money, releasing me to implement the New Start in Life Program. It began in one of the former drug houses that Joy of Jesus renovated. We named the outreach Camden House. It wasn't hard to find the 10 families in the community to work with.

Camden House was established in 1990 to promote healthy human development by empowering families using a holistic approach that intervened to address physical, spiritual and social/emotional needs. Our purpose was to improve the quality of life for welfare-dependent families by providing employability and parenting skills, individual/group therapy, and entrepreneurship; and by teaching and reinforcing concepts to support the family unit. The goal: self-sufficiency.

Our families consisted of over 100 individuals. Sometimes there were multiple generations in the home. The challenges they faced ran the gamut: some were headed by substance abusers (alcohol or drugs), others were plagued by physical or sexual abuse, others had low educational aspirations or expectations, and still others had members who had been or were currently in the criminal justice system. The common thread, however, was poverty.

Sometimes the way you name a thing changes everything. In an effort to change the way these families looked at themselves, and the way we looked at them as well, we called these families "fragile." Not dysfunctional—unable to make their way as a family, fundamentally different from "normal," coming apart at the seams, "crazy"—but fragile—teetering precariously on the edge, delicate, in need of care-full care, or care that is full of care, deserving as a flower is deserving of sun and water, inviting someone to lovingly embrace them despite their challenges.

See the difference? Perception is EVERYTHING.

In the Camden House living room, we had a sign on the wall that said, "We are family." None of us were educated as clinicians. But God gave us the wisdom, knowledge and understanding as to how to treat our families. Quite frankly, the families we worked with taught us a lot about how to help them. The secret to our success is that we demonstrated the love and patience of God towards people who had been rejected, many times for good reasons, by their natural families. We focused a great deal on building or rebuilding their self-esteem.

One of my favorite memories is when we had family photos taken to be placed on the living room end tables at Camden House. One of the families missed the photo session. One day I walked into the room. As I glanced at the table, I noticed that this family had quietly placed their family photo with the rest of the pictures on the end table. '*We are part of the family too,*' the photo seemed to say.

The New Start in Life Program was so successful that we were voted the best out of the ten organizations that received the funding. Although the $50,000 was intended to be a one-time, seed money grant, they gave us another $50,000 for a second follow-up year.

We were able to do this great work with just a few dedicated people. One was Minister Dessie Morgan who came in initially as our Bible study teacher. Because of her outstanding gifts and talents, she became my assistant director and eventually the director when I left Camden House in 1994. We had many other dedicated staff and volunteers including, but not limited to, Deidre Allen Woods, Pastor Alliene Johnson, Elsie Camacho and the late Renee Lowe-Curling, who came in later and served as our staff psychologist. Carolyn Christianson did an outstanding job of keeping us on track in order to fulfill our grant requirements. We also had various interns doing their field work at Camden House. All of them have since gone on to do even greater works.

Because of our success with getting community residents delivered from drugs and alcohol, I was recruited to be a consultant on Capitol Hill in Washington, D.C., where we had been commissioned by Congressman John Conyers from Detroit to study and present *"The Root Causes of Substance Abuse."* This was a two-year assignment and one that I will never forget. I learned things about the secular world that reinforced my steadfast belief that "Jesus is the Answer."

To begin with, I was called by the commission because somehow they had learned of our success at Camden House with getting crack addicts, criminals, and other wayward people free from negative lifestyles and to turn their lives around. I think the recognition we received from the Point of Light Award had something to do with bringing Camden House to the Commission's attention.

The day they called me they asked the question, *"To what to you attribute your success?"* The only response I could give was, *"We treat the men, women and children we work with like our family and not as dysfunctional people. We provide a loving and caring environment. They know we care. We also do a lot of our work with volunteers and limited staff. In essence, we work out of the box."* After listening to my response, I was asked to be a part of the "Root Cause of Substance Abuse" Study in Washington.

I was excited about this opportunity and anxious to share my approach with those with ears to hear. However, it didn't take me long once I arrived in Washington to realize that they were deaf to my insights—especially when I offered for their consideration that the root cause was "Man's separation from God." Sitting at the table were people from all walks of life: psychologists, psychiatrists, social workers, professors, chemists, probations officers, judges, health care professionals...I was the only one present openly representing the spiritual side of man, the only ordained minister.

After being given the initial opportunity to express my stance on the position, I was subsequently and pointedly ignored. On more than one occasion, I would raise my hand to give input and someone else would be called upon to give their opinion. There was no doubt that I was deliberately being slighted.

Interestingly enough, just as Nicodemus came to Jesus at night, during breaks different panelists would come up to me and say how glad they were that I was at the table. One person even told me that his father was a pastor. When I asked, *"Why don't you speak up if you agree?"* he just turned and walked away. I felt like the odd man out. And it didn't help when folks back at home told me that I was wasting my time, *"They don't want to hear what you have to say. Why bother?"* My response was, *"If just one person hears what I have to say and acts accordingly, my time will not have been in vain."* Besides, I was being paid nicely for my time, put up in a lovely hotel room, *and* I needed the break from my trench work at Camden House.

In the end, when the report came out with an overview of the two-year study, there was so much chemical terminology in the manual that it was nearly impossible for a layperson to understand what in the world they were saying in the 200-page report. Bottom line: their conclusion was that the root cause of substance abuse is a "chemical imbalance." When I contacted them to find out if anything I said made the book, I was referred to a certain page in the report when I found a one-liner that said, *"There may be a spiritual connection."*

This experience left me with assurance that Camden House and our "New Start in Life Program," which included an emphasis on spirituality, was the answer to man's addictions. I had this experience nearly 15 years ago, and lo and behold, we are now seeing more and more programs that recognize the truth that man *is* a spirit, *has* a soul and *lives* in a body. We are seeing a new nomenclature that is becoming increasingly popular: "faith-based." We are seeing even secular institutions and individuals attest to the effectiveness of these new programs that place more emphasis on treating the total person: spirit, soul, and body.

Although Camden House was never intended to be a traditional church, many of the Ravendale residents had their first exposure to the deeper things of God by participating in this "New Start in Life" program. I am pleased to be able to say that many of the families enrolled in our program were referred to and became members of Faith Clinic Church Of God In Christ, located across the street from Joy of Jesus. We give tremendous applause to Faith Clinic's first couple, Pastor and Mrs. (Lisa) Zachary Hicks for their fine nurturing of these former Camden House families. Many have gone on to be leaders in this wonderful church.

Some years ago, I received a wonderful tribute from Faith Clinic. They gave me a *"Woman of Excellence Award."* The following is just one of many testimonies of Ravendale residents who experienced this life-changing intervention through Joy of Jesus Ministries.

"Camden House was one of the first places where I discovered who I really am. When I first went to Camden House, I thought it was a place to go to get the things (material) you needed. That was only part of it! To me it was a home away from home. Camden House is where I learned that I can cry all I wanted to and it was alright, because I'm not who I used to be.

"The more I got to know the people there it was like I didn't have to be nobody else. There I found out that I can love myself in spite of myself. That's the one thing I will always thank the counselors at Camden House for helping me to find myself.

"'When I am down and need someone to talk to, I can always go there with or without an appointment. This is something I do a lot, but it has made me strong.

"With the help of God and the people He put in place to help me, I know that I can make it. But I also know that when I need a place to go to that I can always go to Camden House and tell them my problems.

"I thank Mrs. Dessie Morgan who let me cry that river and for letting me know I don't have to be the one to hold everything up. So, Camden House, from the bottom of my heart, I thank you for all your help and love."

S.H., resident

Years later, in 1990, WTVS Channel 56 and WJBK Channel 2 (now the Fox Channel), two Detroit-based stations, did a one-hour documentary about Joy of Jesus called, *"A Neighborhood Redeemed."* They talked about our childhood development center, housing, entrepreneurial and employment training programs. Sadly, they left out the heart: the spiritual aspects of our ministry. During the filming of the documentary, I kept asking when someone would be coming to interview some of the people at Camden House. I never got a good answer. I didn't know that we had been left out until I went to the premiere showing of the documentary. When I realized that such a significant part of the ministry had been omitted, I asked my husband about it. His response was, *"I let them do it their way and I stayed out of it."* My family, friends and Camden House staff was furious. The pain that I felt was incredible. It took some of the joy out of receiving the 107th Point of Light Award for our community outreach work, which was given to us that same year.

Minister Morgan and I are very proud of our former New Start in Life families. We have watched some of their children grow up to become productive citizens of Detroit – and beyond.

Over the years, Joy of Jesus received many awards. However, the one I treasure the most is the *"Others"* Award, given to us by The Salvation Army. It is one of the highest awards they give. We give God all the glory!

Chapter 23

Behind Closed Doors

This is a difficult chapter to write,
but I believe it is necessary.

Therefore I do not run like a man running aimlessly; I do not fight like a man beating the air. No, I beat my body and make it my slave so that after I have preached to others, I myself will not be disqualified for the prize.
1 Cor. 9:26-27

People look at couples in ministry and imagine that their marriages must necessarily be strong. The couples often work very hard publicly to give that impression, and many of these marriages are indeed strong, loving marriages. But I must be honest. My marriage with Eddie was a lot like the marriages that many of you have. Certainly I loved him, and he loved me; but we had our share of troubles and conflicts. Rather than giving a long story, I'm going to open my journal door and let you peek inside. Don't be shocked at what you see.

September 5, 1985

The month of August was hot and very hot. Not so much temperature-wise, but I have been truly tried by the fire in my marriage. It has been three years since our wedding day and not much has changed since our first anniversary. I had to spend our first anniversary alone because Eddie had accepted a dinner speaking engagement on behalf of Joy of Jesus – *for men only!* I spent my wedding anniversary washing clothes. I cried so much that I could have used the water from my tears to wash the clothes. I thought he would never do it again. But he did. On our second wedding anniversary, he accepted another dinner commitment for the ministry. The only difference was that time I got to go!

Eddie's attention has been divided into so many different areas – mostly work, work, work! The first week of our vacation was aborted – again – because of "pressing business" at Joy of Jesus. It came as a hurting surprise to me and I "blew up." Probably did more harm than good. I don't now how to deal with this. This marriage keeps me on my face.

After a cooling off period of two days, I wrote Eddie a long letter and requested a discussion period. We had a talk last night. He feels as if he is doing the best he can and was totally non-committal regarding devoting more time to our marriage. He did state that we can pick up the discussion during our trip to PTL. We leave this Friday. Eddie and I need help. It is my prayer that we will get a new lease on our marriage when we go south.

July 26, 1988

Lord, thank you for the way you are moving by your spirit! Several prayers have been answered in the last few days! Eddie has started back up the Men's Bible Study Class. Today he initiated the Prayer of Agreement with me for a new church home. And we have started back praying together at 6:00 a.m. I am praying for a clear financial slate for the ministry by September 30th.

July 31, 1988

Going to the Raulerson's meeting yesterday was ordained by God. Although I was beat with many stripes it was good for me for I have been disobedient. Again, God has spoken these words to me:

"Why do you look for someone else to do what I have told you to do?"

God reminded me of Moses and how he was called from the burning bush to deliver God's people out of Egypt. Moses felt that he didn't know what to say to the people because he didn't have "eloquent" speech. He also made other excuses not to do what God called him to do. God's anger began to kindle against Moses. In the end, however, he did agree to go and God gave him a teammate, his brother Aaron, to speak to the people as Moses instructed. However, Aaron and Miriam, his sister, later turned against Moses and also turned the people towards rebellion and made the golden calf their god. Very important. Caution.

I have repented to the Lord for disobedience and will now do what He has called me to do – deliver the oppressed.

Bill Raulerson spoke some prophetic words (profound and beautiful) over me. He has confirmed my calling: I am an evangelist in the body of Christ. I will walk worthy of the profession to which I have been called – with God's help.

August 1, 1988

At times, it seems that Eddie and I are unequally yoked. Through prayer, God has revealed that we are not. Both of us have been called to the same work – deliverance. Eddie to natural deliverance and I to spiritual deliverance. The problem is that we have not respected each others gifts and callings and esteemed one another above ourselves.

My perception has changed. Heretofore, I have felt that God has only called Eddie to change the city of Detroit and that my job was to help his vision come to pass. However, I am reminded that man shall not live by bread alone but by every word that comes from the mouth of God. Therefore, we must focus on the total man – spirit, soul and body.

I must help Eddie, but he must also help me. How do I want him to help me?

1) Openly appoint me to the position of director of spiri-

tual development. By doing this, I will become spiritually accountable to the people and this position will get the respect and support it needs to grow.

2) That I will be relieved of all other administrative responsibilities that are not in accordance with God's will for me.

Selah: *It is important to name what you want from your spouse. Your spouse is a human being, NOT a mind-reader! I cannot tell you the freedom I gained from doing that—without anger, just saying what you want.*

August 6, 1988

Thursday night God poured out His spirit on my Ladies Bible Study Class. Women seemed to come from everywhere: Taylor, Grosse Pointe, the far, far west side of Detroit, Highland Park, and Ravendale. They came in twos and threes. Things started off slowly with just Debbie and me and then two new sisters came from the west side. After that, they poured in. There were 15, including me. Most were new. We had <u>two</u> praise and worship leaders. Truly, God is answering prayer. Every time I get down to only one or two students, He starts things all over again. It is my desire to continue.

June 7, 1990

1 + 1 = 1.

Math has always been a challenge for me, as you can see. But math isn't my only challenge. Lately my marriage has been an even greater challenge.

God gave me a vision for my marriage nearly eight years ago when my husband and I were married. Scripture tells us that the two shall become one in marriage; that was the theme for our wedding. Unfortunately, however, as our community outreach ministry has increased, our marital relationship has decreased. More and more programs, more and more people, more and more busyness have come between my husband and I. As a result, 1 + 1 equals 11, which equals trouble.

No matter how you add it up, unless that third party is the Lord, (who should be in the middle of all marriages) there can be little hope for the future.

I am reminded of another scripture that says, *"Where there is no vision, the people perish* (Proverbs 29:18a)." Such is the case with my marriage. Where there is no vision, the marriage perishes. I have heard Eddie say more than once, *"Mary has always had more vision for our marriage than I have."*

Nevertheless, I have sought the Lord for a renewed vision for my marriage. He has encouraged me to do the following:

One: fast and pray; two: humble myself under His mighty hand and in due season He will exalt me AND our marriage.

Finally, the Lord has reassured me that 1 + 1 still equals 1 and although it may tarry, it will come to pass. I have written the vision. So let it be.

Prayer: Lord, help me to walk by faith and not by sight.

Selah: *Sometimes we pray and pray and wait...and after two months, we expect, CERTAINLY the Lord should be making a "mighty move." It doesn't always work that way—in marriage or in any area of life. That's what this next journal entry is about. It's important that we do as Jesus commanded: "PRAY, but also WATCH" (Matt. 26:41). In the entry below, I describe the experience of "watching"—that is, doing some real soul-searching work to uncover the root of our marital challenges. Marriage is work ALL the time!*

August 27, 1990

My marriage to Eddie is at a very critical stage. With all of my heart, I believe that God planned this union and He intended for it to glorify Him. He gifted us with each other. He knew what I needed and He knew what Eddie needed. The problem is that we haven't learned to accept each other and respect one another's God-given talents and spiritual gifts.

Eddie is a visionary. He is also very task-oriented. I have attempted to get him to be my spiritual leader and I have become frustrated with my lack of success. In turn, he has become resentful with my attempts.

Selah: *What exactly did I mean by "spiritual leader?" Sometimes we get caught up in an image of what we think we want, when God* *has what we need right in front of us and we fail to see it. God help us to take our blinders off, and prayerfully consider what He might be doing when we think He's not hearing our prayers!*

On the other hand, I am a shepherd girl and my calling is to feed the sheep and sit at the feet of Jesus. For the past seven years, I feel that Eddie has forced me to be a "Martha" and busy myself with tasks to further his vision. I have become frustrated and resentful with his attempts and his successes at persuasion.

As a result of this tense situation, God is revealing some lessons to me.

Lesson #1 – Let all things be done in moderation.
Lesson #2 – Let your light shine everywhere.
Lesson #3 – Cease from your labors and enter into God's rest.
Lesson #4 – When we are men-pleasers, we can't please God.
Lesson #5 – "The Way of Cain."

Here are some lessons that I took from this pivotal story in the book of Genesis, where Cain, the world's first son, kills younger brother Abel after God accepts Abel's animal sacrifice offering but not Cain's offering of the "fruit of the land." Essentially, I take from this story that Cain wants to do things his way and not God's way; and that, no matter how legitimate you think your actions and activities are, they mean *nothing* if they're not of God.

1) I've been so busy doing "Eddie's thing" that I've forgotten how to do God's thing.

2) I've resented Eddie for his lack of appreciation.

3) I've been so busy doing man's thing that I haven't had time to:

-Go to church to be nurtured

-Clean my house

-Rest

4) As Cain was jealous of Abel, I've been jealous of those who receive Eddie's praise.

5) Abel was a keeper of the flock. He fed the sheep. He gave God his best. God gave Abel his gift (sheep) and Abel gave them back to God.

6) The best that I can give God is to feed His sheep.

7) Abel loved his sheep, (God loved His only Son) yet he gave a sacrificial offering. (God gave His only Son.).

8) Abel showed his appreciation to God by giving his best.

9) Cain gave out of his abundance. Abel gave out of his need.

10) Cain gave God his leftovers. I've been giving God whatever attention I could after doing man's will.

11) God blessed Cain with all the earth and a great harvest. Cain had an ungrateful spirit.

12) Cain did not have a sense of sin and did not feel that he needed to make a blood sacrifice.

13) Cain was a type of anti-christ. Abel was a type of Christ.

14) Cain was the first to start a new civilization without God. He built the first city and named it Enoch, new beginning.

15) Cain's city and kingdom were the beginning of the world kingdom that renounced God.

February 14, 2001

The Holy Spirit has spoken to me through several of His people. Woe unto me. I have broken one of God's commandments – the first one. *"Thou shalt have no other God's before me" (Ex. 20:3)*. I truly love the Lord and it was hard for me to believe that I could be breaking this most important of commandments. Here's what I see:

Eddie goes to bed early (9:00 p.m.) There are spiritual things that I could have done after 9:00 p.m. However, because I desired to be with my husband in bed watching movies, I left the Lord for my husband. The Lord didn't get first place. He is a jealous God and has not been pleased with this rejection. I, who have felt rejection so many times over the years, have rejected Him.

Ouch. For a long time, I have accused my husband of not having his priorities right. But I am just as guilty; maybe more so.

God has blessed me with a good husband. But like the children of Israel when they were blessed leaving Egypt with golden earrings and other "spoils," they later made a god out of them in the wilderness. It appears that I have taken God's blessing and made a god out of it.

My spirit is convicted. I have asked God's forgiveness—and Eddie's. I shared with him that we were both putting other things before God. Plus, I asked Eddie's forgiveness for putting a burden on him by expecting him to meet my needs. God alone is able.

Because I felt Eddie wasn't meeting my needs emotionally and spiritually, I had built up some anger and resentment towards him, especially when I was sick. I felt that he should have been more sensitive and prayed more for me.

This is a lonely time for me. When Eddie goes to bed at 9:00 p.m., I am still up for hours. I'm realizing that God wants intimacy with me. So: I will rendezvous with Him. During that time, I will pray for those on our prayer list.

When Job prayed for his friends, his change came.
(Job 42:10)

October 11, 2002

Today is my birthday. I woke up this morning with the infirmed on my mind. So many of my family and friends are sick. I sense that my 21-day fast for the sick must start before November 1st.

October 13, 2002

On Sunday, I went to a church on Detroit's west side for Women's Day. I didn't know the speaker and she didn't know me. But, praise the Lord, her message was: "Has Anyone Seen Mary?"

The songstress was also a visiting guest. She sang: "Mary's Alabaster Box." How blessed I was. This was my birthday present from the Lord!

October 16, 2002

I have been celebrating my birthday all week. My 60th birthday this year has been my most memorable. Eddie held my party at the Shangri-La Restaurant in West Bloomfield, Michigan. There were 50-60 guests in attendance. Many wonderful remarks were given by close friends.

However, my gift from Eddie took my mind off of the sad things going on. My gift from Eddie for our 20th wedding anniversary, which is today—an Alabaster Box!

My other gift was the gift of words. My good friend Debby Mitchell wrote a poem for me. *"I see you as the watch-*

woman on the wall," she said. Here is the poem:

Watchwoman

For Mary Edwards on her 60th Birthday
(October 11, 2002)

Watch woman
O Watchwoman on the wall
Wailing before the Lord
Interceding for His people

Watchwoman
Oh watchwoman
What do you see?
What do you hear?
What saith the Lord?

Watchwoman
Oh watch woman
Wailing
Wailing
Looking over the city
Sounding the alarm.
Warning the people
Saddened by sin
Angered by injustice
Dismayed by the apathy

Watchwoman
O watchwoman
Moaning
Groaning
Tossing and turning
What saith the Lord?

What's in store for His people?
What danger lies ahead?
What prosperity is in store?

Watchwoman
Oh watchwoman
Pounding out the warnings
Typing out the truth
Being a voice to the voiceless
Saying what others dare not say
Standing bold in the righteousness of God

Watchwoman
Oh Watchwoman
What do you see?
What do you hear?
What sayeth the Lord?
Laboring
Delivering
Birthing dreams
Seeing visions
Standing tall among women
Yet humble in spirit

Watchwoman
O Watchwoman
What lies in store for you?
Great things
Far greater
Far greater
Than yet we've seen
The latter years
Far greater than
The former years
So thus says the Lord

Watchwoman
Oh Watchwoman
Your future is sure
There is an expected end
There is a garment of praise for your
Heaviness
There is new joy each morning

Watchwoman
O Watchwoman
What do you see
What do you hear?
What saith the Lord?

Cry out
Shout loud
Be bold
Don't hold back
Watchwoman
O Watchwoman
For this cause you were born
Watch woman
O Watchwoman
What saith the Lord?

It is my hope that these frank revelations will encourage you. Good marriages are full of surprises, contradictions, and yes, conflict. What is important here is that we stayed true and faithful to one another; we loved each other through the dry places, through the questions, through the disagreements.

All's well that ends well.
Shakespeare

My dear husband wasn't very good at expressing himself in a romantic way with his own words. But he always gave me the most beautiful cards. I have a collection of all of his cards. There's no doubt in my mind that he loved me.

Eddie and I did indeed end well. In fact, seven months before he died, our church at the time, Evangel Ministries in Detroit, Michigan, named us *"Couple of the Year"* in 2004. We finished the business we had with each other. You'll see when you read *"Get Your House In Order"* in Chapter 27.

The late Elder James E. Slappy (standing left) with Minister Mary and Rev. Eddie K. Edwards. Missionary Claudette Slappy (seated)

Pastors James and Alice Pittman, Dayspring Church, Windsor, Ontario, Canada with Minister Mary.

Chapter 24

The Called and Ready Writers

...be ready always to give an answer to every man that asketh you a reason of the hope that is in you...
1 Pet. 3:15b

For many years, I worked diligently by the side of my late, great husband, helping him to fulfill his vision for the city of Detroit, particularly the Ravendale Community on the east side. I used every gift and talent that I had, and some I didn't even know that I had—until I got in the trenches!

I have always said that I *"married into the Joy of Jesus Ministries."* And, indeed, I did. When I married Rev. Edwards, the ministry had already begun their outreach to youngsters through their summer camp and after school programs, which I described earlier. I guess those "$2.00 notes" that I had to take to the neighbors when I was a child, borrowing money for us to eat, was a part of my preparation for the Joy of Jesus Ministries.

As the development director, I helped my husband raise over one million dollars every year for at least the ten years that I was in that position. I had to do many things that I didn't particularly enjoy, but they were necessary in order for us to build up the Kingdom of God. In the meantime, however, I longed to pursue my writing ministry, which had been in my heart for over 30 years before I met my husband.

One Christmas, back in the late 70s, I was broke. Christmas was approaching, and I had no money to purchase gifts for my family and friends. Upon sharing my *"woe is me"* story with the Lord, His response was, *"What are you going to do with what you have in your hands?"* What He was referring to was the proverbial shoeboxes of writings that had been accumulating for years under my bed, in the closets, in the attic, and in my dresser drawers. To make a long story short, I pulled them out, typed them up, my friend drew my cover, I put them in a book, and gave them as Christmas presents. My family and friends were overjoyed with the creativity of my gift and they shared my book, *Morning Papers,* with their friends. In turn, others wanted it. And, before I knew what was happening, I was selling books left and right. I was in the book publishing business, using a gift that God had deposited within me as a very young girl.

As a young girl living in an incredibly challenging environment, I used to write in my diary how I wanted my life to be instead of the way it really was. Praise the Lord. Today I have seen some of that come true.

"For the vision is yet for an appointed time, but at the end it shall speak, and not lie; though it tarry, wait for it; because it will surely come; it will not tarry"
(Hab. 2:3)

By the time I began ministry at Joy of Jesus, I had written two books:

Morning Papers, the devotional book mentioned above, and *The Fish Market*, my personal salvation testimony, which included evangelism tips. I knew that I had more books inside of me, but the ministry didn't allow me the opportunity to write them. The only writing I was doing at Joy of Jesus was grant writing, fundraising appeal letters, and the Joy of Jesus newsletter. However, in 1984, God heard my cry to pursue my passion to write and He blessed me to pen some of my experiences in the Ravendale Community by publishing *Mary, Don't You Weep.* This small book of poetry described what it was like to live in Ravendale and reach out to that impoverished community. After publishing this book, I formed a personal writing ministry called Joyful Heart Ministries, which quickly expanded.

Once people began to realize that I had a gift for writing, they started approaching me to help them write their books. At that point, in addition to my regular duties at Joy of Jesus, I became a book coach and did my best to squeeze this new ministry into my very busy schedule. I also managed to work in a writers' conference in June of 2000. It was held at the Salvation Army Headquarters in Southfield, Michigan. This was a memorable day. It was the day I met a very special lady who would become a significant part of my writing ministry.

The first time I saw her I knew that she was a gift from God. The determined look on her face told me that she was about the Father's business. The wide-brim summer straw hat bounced on her head as she stalked the Salvation Army where the writers' seminar was to be held. There was no one else around but the two of us.

"Are you here for the seminar?" I asked. *"Yes, I am,"* she responded with a somewhat irritated look on her face. *"But I have walked around this entire building, all of the doors are locked and I can't get it."*

Wanda Burnside had arrived early; that's why the doors weren't open. Just about that time the maintenance man came with the keys to let us in.

"Can I help you with those things?" Wanda asked as she watched me open up the trunk of my car to retrieve items for the seminar. It was obvious that God had sent her because I had no other help. The two of us began to haul the materials into the center. That was the beginning of our wonderful, long-term relationship and the beginning of Wanda Burnside helping me with "those things."

Although only 17 people had signed up in advance to attend the conference, 20 more came to the door. We ended up with more than twice the number of people I had prepared for. But, together, we pulled it off and got everyone seated.

Following the seminar, an evaluation was given to the attendees asking, *"Would you be interested in doing this again?"* Without exception, everyone said yes. Little did I know then that what I thought would be a one-time seminar turned into years of ministry under the name *"The Called and Ready Writers" (CRW)*. Call (313) 491-3504 or visit CRW at www.thecalledandreadywriters.org.

With Wanda Burnside by my side, we have spent years fulfilling our mission statement:

"To educate and encourage both aspiring and published writers to use their gift of communications to spread the glorious gospel of Jesus Christ to Christians and non-Christians alike, and to leave an inheritance for their children's children."

Our foundational scriptures are from Jeremiah 30:1-2:

"This is the word that came to Jeremiah from the Lord: This is what the Lord, the God of Israel says, Write in a book all the words I have spoken to you;"

...and from Proverbs 13:22a:

"A good man leaves an inheritance for his children's children."

We have had numerous writers come through the Guild since 1998. Some stay longer than others. As I grow older, I have learned how to sit back and enjoy my fruit. I did that recently when I attended a CRW meeting. Wanda was displaying the talents of our legendary authors at a special book-signing event. I want to take this opportunity to publicly salute them: Minister Dorothy Butler, Mr. John Butler, Mrs. Dorothy Kimble, Elder Minor Palm, Jr., and Mr. William Kuykendall. Keep being fruitful. The Bible tells us in Psalm 92:14 that *"They will still bear fruit in old age; they will stay fresh and green."*

Wanda Burnside took the presidency mantle from me on January 1, 2006. She has done a superb job of leading this ministry. I want to thank Wanda and her current board of directors for their hard work and for keeping the mission of CRW alive.

I also want to thank Mrs. Karen Love, CEO of both the Michigan Chronicle and the Michigan Front Page, two prestigious African American publications, for allowing me an opportunity to write a weekly inspirational column for three years in their newspapers. Because of the great response received from their readers, I was encouraged to publish two of my books, *At His Feet* and *Ponderings from the Heart of Mary*, using these columns. This open door also led me to publish

M.E.D.I.C. Ministries magazine, using columns from these two publications. More about this communications outreach in Chapter 26.

Chapter 25

His Lovely Wife Ministries

Who can find a virtuous woman? For her price is far above rubies. The heart of her husband doth safely trust in her, so that he shall have no need of spoil.
Prov. 31:10-11

My girlfriend Peggy is married to the mayor of a small but prosperous town in New Jersey. One day Peggy and her husband were walking down the street of their town and heard a voice cry out, *"Peggy, Peggy."* Peggy and the mayor stopped and turned around. Up on a scaffold was a man washing windows. *"Who's that man calling your name, Peggy?"* The mayor asked. *"Oh, that's Joe, my old boyfriend,"* Peggy responded. With a smug look on his face, the mayor said, *"Aren't you glad you married me? If you had married him, you would be the wife of a window washer."* Peggy's response spoke volumes. Demurely, she replied, *"No, dear. If*

I had married him, HE would be the mayor."

I like to tell this story whenever I'm invited to churches by the first lady to speak to her audience. Truly, I can relate to my friend Peggy. This is the way that I felt when we received the 107th Point of Light award spoken of earlier in chapter twenty-two, "From Camden House to the White House."

Too often, those behind the scenes, especially the pastor's wife, receive so little appreciation, recognition or praise, while the man out front receives all the applause. For this reason, I felt a pull on my heartstrings to establish a support group for pastors' wives and other women in spiritual leadership. This group would provide them with an opportunity to vent some of their frustration in a safe environment. The mission of this 501(c)3 organization would be to "educate, encourage, and embrace women in spiritual leadership, thereby enhancing their lives."

Although I had this inspiration in 1990, like so many of my other visions, I had to wait until 1998 for it to be launched. Perhaps you heard us over Radio Station WLQV and WMUZ broadcasting our program, "Ask The Pastor's Wife." Each Saturday afternoon we had various pastors' wives from around the Metropolitan Detroit Area come on the program to be interviewed about their challenges as first ladies in their churches. I want to thank Pastor Renaye Coles of Peaceful Waters Ministries, for her excellent leadership as president of His Lovely Wife Ministries during its early days.

This support group ministry was happening simultaneously with the establishment of The Called and Ready Writers. Throughout my ministry, I've always had more than one initiative going on at the same time. To God be the glory! I truly know that without Him I can do nothing. But with Him, all things are possible.

I want to thank Ministers Otto and Wendy Tucker for their faithful commitment to all of my ministries over the years. They did the logos for both The Called and Ready Writers and His Lovely Wife Ministries, as well as designed the cover for M.E.D.I.C. magazine. Not only have they lent their creative talents, but they have given us their financial support monthly for years. Wendy served in the past as the secretary for His Lovely Wife Ministries. The couple now resides in Savannah, Georgia and work diligently in their home church there.

Under the auspices of His Lovely Wife Ministries, I launched a magazine called "M.E.D.I.C," an acronym for Manifesting Entire Deliverance in Christ. As Christians, we should be concerned about the total person: spirit, soul and body. In the next chapter, you will learn about the impact of that magazine.

Chapter 26

M.E.D.I.C. Magazine

(Manifesting Entire Deliverance in Christ)

For this purpose, the son of man was manifested to destroy the works of the devil.
1 John 3:8

Little did I know when I accompanied my husband to The Rose of Sharon Church Of God In Christ in Detroit, Michigan, on November 17, 2002, that I would be birthing a new ministry. Eddie had been requested by Rev. Ronald Griffin to deliver the morning message on this particular day, and I would become "pregnant"—with spiritual vision.

I was delighted to sit in the front row of the church with charming First Lady Linda Griffin. We hit it off right away, bonding immediately in the spirit. When I look back, I can see that this was God-ordained because of what was about to take place.

In the midst of Eddie's message, Pastor Griffin put a buzz in his ear informing him that they were going to have an impromptu baptism. 21-year old LaMonica Molette, who was a member of the church, had left the Barbara Ann Karmanos Cancer Institute Center at Harper Hospital that morning and insisted on being water baptized that day. LaMonica had leukemia and it was in its final stages. About four or five of her family members were being baptized with her.

Because of her weak condition and the need to stay warm, Eddie was asked to bring his message to an abrupt close. Being very sensitive to the request and the need of the moment, he was glad to do so.

Shortly thereafter, in walks LaMonica under her own steam. It was initially thought that she would need to be wheeled in. But no: LaMonica said, *"I'm walking in."* And she did, followed by four or five family members.

Together they were all baptized at The Rose of Sharon Church Of God In Christ. One by one they entered the baptism pool as an outward declaration of their faith in Jesus Christ (Mark 16:16). LaMonica was the youngest one to declare her faith in her family that day.

"And a little child shall lead them" (Isaiah 11:6).

As I watched the baptism, I noticed a young man videotaping each one going into the pool and as they came out. The voice of the Lord spoke to my heart and said, *"Tell the church to get ready for a wedding and not a funeral."* My heart nearly skipped a beat as I turned with excitement to Sister Griffin and repeated what I had heard. This added an extra element of jubilation to the excitement she was already experiencing because of the family baptism.

Sister Griffin left the sanctuary to assist LaMonica with the removal of her wet clothes. *"Oh, Lord,"* I said within, *"please allow me the opportunity to pray for this young lady."* Within a few minutes, an usher came to get me. I was taken to LaMonica. In the room were a number of other women, including Sister Griffin, Barbara Davis, LaMonica's mother, and Marion Pierre, her paternal grandmother.

"Tell these ladies what the Lord said to you in the sanctuary," Sister Griffin said.

I repeated what I had been told. LaMonica and everyone in the room nearly shrieked with joy! My prayer was answered and I had an opportunity to minister to LaMonica, build up the faith of those in the room to believe God for a miracle, and then pray and lay hands on LaMonica.

Within minutes of concluding the prayer, in walks

George. George was the young man doing videotaping in the sanctuary. I didn't know at the time that this was LaMonica's boyfriend.

Guess what he came to do? Propose! Propose to LaMonica on his knees, no less. This moment was captured on video camera for the world to see. LaMonica said, *"Yes."* We all marveled at how radiant she appeared.

Later, when I was alone, the Lord continued to speak to me. *"Without a vision, my people perish"* (Prov. 29:18). LaMonica needed a vision of life, not death.

The following week I was at LaMonica's blood drive where 253 people turned out to give blood. Many people, including LaMonica, were wearing T-shirts saying, *"LaMonica's Miracle Blood Drive."* At the bottom of the shirt, there was a line: *"I gave blood, did you?"*

There's another bottom line: Jesus gave his blood on Calvary for all mankind, including LaMonica. He had already given her a spiritual transfusion. It was a perfect match, one made in heaven. She said "yes" to more than George. She said "yes" to Jesus Christ. LaMonica had now become His bride, the bride of Christ. Like George wanted to be, He is her Bridegroom.

Barbara Howard, a good friend of the church's first lady, was also a visitor there that day. After the service, Ms.

Howard approached me, introduced herself, and asked if I might be able to help with a mission for which she had great passion. She began to describe the tremendous need among African Americans suffering from leukemia to receive bone marrow transplants. Ms. Howard had been a donor and was now deeply committed to sharing this crisis need with others. *"I've never been married or given birth to any children,"* she said, *"but I do know what it is to give life to another human being, as a result of becoming a bone marrow donor."*

I knew very little about the great need myself, so I asked Barbara to send me some information. She did, and the first story about LaMonica came out in the *Michigan Front Page* on December 13, 2002. It was called *LaMonica's Spiritual Transfusion.* A couple of months later, during Black History Month in February of 2003, I wrote a story for the *Michigan Front Page* about four patients in the Detroit area who were waiting and praying for a matching bone marrow donor. Once my eyes were opened, I felt a need to do more. This led to me coalescing four churches and a beauty salon to do bone marrow drives. We found over 80 potential donors. To God be the glory!

Unfortunately, none of them were a match for LaMonica. On February 23, 2003, LaMonica passed away—unfortunately, before she and George had a chance to wed. But don't be discouraged. Our faith, our belief in God's ability, our obedience to Him, is never, ever in vain. We'll never know the depth of joy that LaMonica and George experienced that day of his proposal. We'll never know the impact that day had on any one individual present to witness the incredibly bold and risky act that George took to ask a "dying" woman to marry him.

You know how our ancestors always say that when someone dies, another one is born? That happened with La-Monica. Not that a baby was born, but the Lord used her to give birth to a new ministry – *M.E.D.I.C.: Manifesting Entire Deliverance in Christ.* The articles in the *Michigan Front Page* and the bone marrow drives led me to publish *M.E.D.I.C.* magazine. This magazine helped to fulfill the mission of *His Lovely Wife Ministries,* which had been founded as a 501(c) (3) organization in 1998. We are dedicated to enhancing the lives of women in spiritual leadership with education, encouragement and embracing. Subsequent issues of *M.E.D.I.C.* magazine covered information about sickle cell anemia, alopecia and leukemia. The magazine was one of the tools God used to open the eyes of many of us to do more to reach out to those in need.

Barbara Howard wrote this testimony about her experience as a bone marrow donor. I pray that it will encourage you to do the same.

Barbara Howard's Testimony

Since my donation in October of 2000, I've had the opportunity to speak at several bone marrow drives. Most of these have been for children. Recently I discovered that the last drive I did for a little girl was too late. She passed because a donor could not be found. Too many little girls, little boys, young men and women are dying because we as a community are not doing our part. There are approximately 3000 patients searching the registry for a donor each year. We have the resources within our own community to help many more people.

Actually, my story is a very simple one. I signed up for the registry in 1995 while attending an Expo in Cobo Hall. I noticed a sign that said 1-800-MARROW2, and asked a nurse what this was about. She said that it was a national databank of potential donors. These donors are matched with sick persons worldwide who need bone marrow donors. She explained that if a family donor cannot be found, the registry is the next place to search. Even though I didn't understand the process, I signed up anyway, gave them a test tube of blood, and went on my way. I really didn't think much about it.

After five years, my mother got a call from American Red Cross. "They think you're a match," she told me. On August 3, 2000, I made one of the most important call backs of my life.

"This is Barbara Howard," I told the coordinator who answered the phone. "Yes Ms. Howard," she answered, "we need to do some more testing of your blood. We think your marrow is a good match for one of our patients. Will you come in as soon as possible?"

From the moment the coordinator spoke, I knew that I was a match. Without hesitation I said yes. I knew from that moment on that God had something for me to do.

The National Bone Marrow Donor Program matched me with a 29-year-old African American male with acute leukemia.

At this point in his treatment, a bone marrow transplant was his last hope. I don't think I stopped crying for the entire preparation period. I cried not out of fear but out of sheer joy. Imagine me, a lowly servant chosen by God as a vessel of healing. Wow, what an honor! So I went through a very extensive physical. Had my blood checked several times and even had a one-on-one session with my coordinator regarding the process and the aftermath. And because he was in such need, to prepare for collection, I donated two pints of my own blood in an unusually short period of time.

I didn't realize just how emotional this experience was going to be. Nor did I fully understand the impact I was having on someone else's life. Sure, I knew this could help him. I understood that he had few options. But I didn't realize that this act of mine was going to save his life, even if only for a short time.

On October 19th, 2000 at 9:30 a.m., God and I went in the operating room at the University of Michigan and I gave a quart of marrow which was collected, packaged, and placed on a plane. And I was at home by 3:00 in the afternoon. My hips were sore for a couple of weeks, but that was the extent of my discomfort.

I often wondered about this young man unknown to me. I wondered if the transplant worked. I wondered how my marrow was treating him. When I got my first report that the transplant was a success, I cried a river. And I thanked God. I knew it would be successful because I had been praying myself, and been prayed for and prayed over. My blood was fortified!

On December 27, 2001, I found out my recipient lived in St. Louis. His name was Willie. At 6:00 p.m. on the 27th of December, I spoke to him on the phone for the first time. He had married his girlfriend in October, just a few days shy of the one-year anniversary of my marrow donation. They have three children and were adjusting to life after the transplant. He had several bouts with something called "graft vs. host disease," which is a complication that can damage a recipient's organs in any number of ways. He wasn't 100 percent better but he was ALIVE! He wouldn't have been if I hadn't signed up for the registry. He wouldn't have married if I had said no when the Red Cross called me.

Post script: *Willie Harrison died on May 5, 2002, 533 days after his transplant. At first I was devastated. My heart was broken because I felt that somehow I had failed him. On the other hand, because I was available, Willie received additional time with his family. He got a chance to enjoy life a little more. I thank God that He has put me in a position to tell others about His goodness and share with them my life-giving experience. I still say that given the opportunity, I would do this again, without hesitation, without a doubt.*

We could save many more lives if everyone in good health between the ages of 18-60 would sign up. I'm asked all the time if I would ever do this again. My answer is always yes, without hesitation, without a doubt.

May God Himself, the God of peace, sanctify you through and through (wholly). May your whole spirit, soul and body be kept blameless at the coming of our Lord Jesus Christ. The one who called you is faithful and he will do it.
1 Thess. 5:23-24

For more information about becoming a bone marrow donor, contact 1-800-MARROW2.

Chapter 27

Getting Your House in Order

...if you are offering your gift at the altar
and there remember that your brother has
something against you, leave your gift there in
front of the altar. First go and be reconciled to your
brother; then come offer your gift.
Matt. 5:23-24

In December 2003, The Holy Spirit gave me the following words of encouragement:

In 2004 the Eagles Will Soar
© 2003 M. D. Edwards
The is the hour Of God's Supernatural Power
Upon His eagle saints, He will pour
Into high places they will soar

Because of their visionary eye,
They will fly, high, high
Over troops they will leap
And tread upon all that creeps

They will not be burnt when they
Walk through the fire
Proving again and again that

Satan is a liar

When they pass through the waters

They will not drown

For them the King of Kings
Has a victor's crown

Their purposes they will achieve
From the Master's side they will never leave

Each step they take will be an expression

Of their trust in Him
Their Eagle Eye

Will never grow dim

They will succeed because
Their vision is keen

And the breastplate of righteousness
Will keep us all clean

After receiving such an encouraging prophecy, I entered 2004 with high expectations. Desiring to move to Texas, Eddie and I began to look for a home there. It didn't take long for us to find a lovely one in the Kerrville, Texas area. We began to negotiate on the purchase, pending the sale of our Detroit home. We rushed back and put our home on the market.

In February, Eddie began to complain about having a pain in his side. The doctor diagnosed it as an infection and gave him a prescription for antibiotics. In the same month, I had made a commitment to be a reader and a judge for the very first *Chicken Soup for the African American Soul* book. It was difficult for me to find enough quiet time at home to do the reading, so some friends in Texas suggested that I come there. Eddie seemed not to be getting any better. I didn't want to leave him at home alone, but he insisted that I go. I went, and it was an experience that I will never forget.

My friends in Texas, Richard and Lorraine Lémon, arranged for me to lodge with a missionary couple, The Geroys, who had a guesthouse in the rear of their home. Richard picked me up from the airport. We stopped to get groceries, and he took me to the Geroy's home.

I should have known right away that God was up to something when I saw the sign outside of the cabin. It read "Mt. Horeb House." Mt. Horeb was also called Mt. Sinai. Mt. Sinai is where God gave Moses the Ten Commandments. (Ex. 19:20; 20:1-17). Like Moses, God called me to another *"Mt. Horeb,"* where He gave me a *"word fitly spoken."*

A word fitly spoken is like is like apples of gold in pictures of silver.
Prov. 25:11

Mt. Horeb is the place where God called me aside to prepare me for what was up ahead.

There were about 450 pages of submissions that I had to read and recommend. I was to be in Texas for a week, and thought it would take me that long to read it. How wrong I was. God had a lot more on His mind.

Upon entering Mt. Horeb House, the first thing I noticed is that there was no television. That wasn't too upsetting because I'm more of a music listener. However, when I turned on the radio, there was so much static that it was difficult to hear. *"That's okay,"* I said to myself. *"I have my handy-dandy walkman radio."* To my chagrin, after about one hour of listening to my radio, the batteries went dead! Now what? Here I am, out in the country, with no car, no way to get to the store, and my friends are all miles away. There was nothing left to do but read, read and read some more.

After a whole day of reading, I decided to go outside and take a walk. But when I stepped outside, the neighbor's dog across the way wouldn't let me get any further than the front yard of my hosts' home. Behind the house was nothing but woods. I was under house arrest!

After three days, I had completed the Chicken Soup manuscript reading. *"What will I do for the next four days?"* I asked myself, who happened to be the only one around—or so I thought.

Suddenly, I recalled with great joy that I had a deck of cards in my luggage. Fortunately, I had become accustomed to always packing a deck of cards whenever I traveled. Spreading the deck of cards out on the table, I began to play Solitaire. The reason most people like to play Solitaire is because it's a real challenge—hard to win. Well, surprisingly enough, I won the first game. *"Wow! I won! I won!"* I shouted aloud. *"Let me play again."* I couldn't believe what happened next. I won! I won the second game in a row. Hurriedly, I shuffled and laid out the cards for the third game. Well, to my great disappointment, I lost—right away.

But my disappointment quickly changed to great joy when I realized that I had company. I heard the familiar voice of the Lord speaking:

"Beloved, rejoice. You are not alone. And when it looks like you are losing, you are really winning. Look at these cards. There is only one King of Hearts. That's Me. There is only one Queen of Hearts. That's you. The joker (Satan) is not wild. I have him under control. I have an Ace in the hole. Play the cards you are dealt and know that you have a winning hand."

After these words, the Lord instructed me to go into the closet and pray. I literally went into the walk-in closet in the lodge, got down on my face and prayed and prayed and prayed. During that time, the Lord told me to *"go home and get your house in order."* I didn't know what that meant until I arrived back home.

The real estate agent we worked with felt sure our home would sell quickly. We were all surprised when 30 people looked at the home, expressed their love for it, but not one person put a bid on it. Thank God they didn't. In March, Eddie was diagnosed with fourth stage cancer and given only six months to live.

On July 20th, the night before my husband went into Providence Hospital, I got down before him on my knees. *"Please forgive me for anything I've done to offend you,"* I asked him. A tear formed in my eyes as I thought about the disagreements and little conflicts. Every argument, every time I felt slighted about some little thing or other, seemed so unimportant now.

Eddie looked back at me. The only words he was able to form were the words for which my soul had prayed: *"I forgive you."*

There is nothing—nothing!—quite like forgiveness. Think back to when you became a Christian, especially if you gave your life to Christ as an adult. Just think about the freedom you felt when you realized that your sins had been forgiven. Maybe the preacher said that God would remove your sins "as far as the east is from the west." Maybe he or she said that God saves "from the guttermost to the uttermost." Or maybe they just asked the simple question, *"Do you want to be made whole?"* as Jesus asked the lame man by the pool of Bethesda (John 5:1-16). But the one thing you probably remember is that you were very, very grateful.

It's the same when another person forgives you. And nothing can describe what happens when your spouse of 21 years says those three soul-filling words. Afterwards, there was only one thing to do. What do you do when you commemorate the forgiveness of sins? You celebrate! I served us both Holy Communion. It was the first time I had done that. Little did I know that night would be the last, and in fact our last verbal communication together.

Eddie went into the hospital on Wednesday, July 21st, 2004. The doctors took one look at him, and called Hospice Care the next day. Eddie never came back home.

That Saturday night, I was led by the Lord to spend the night alone with my husband. I sat up most of the night professing my love and appreciation to him for the things he had done for me, as well as for others. I also forgave him for the things he should have done but didn't do. Much of the night was spent in prayer, reading the scriptures to him. One of Eddie's favorite scriptures was from Isaiah 58:12(KJV);

"And they that shall be of thee shall build the old waste places; thou shalt raise up the foundations of many generations; and thou shall be called the repairer of the breach. The restorer of paths to dwell in."

This was his focus throughout his ministry, along with Nehemiah 8:10b (KJV).

"For the joy of the Lord is your strength."

I also played one of his favorite CDs: Richard Smallwood's *"Healing: Live in Detroit."* Some of the songs from the recording sort of summed up Eddie's life and latter days:

"I Love You, Lord"
"Glorify the Lord"
"Center of My Joy"
"Total Praise"
"Thank You"
"Angels Watching Over Me"

Although he was only half-conscious, I felt that he knew I was there.

We had had a full marriage and here we were together, alone, and full once again. My crying this time wasn't uncontrollable. It was quiet. The tears were for everything: the good and bad, the love and passion that kept us, the first time we met, the prophetic words the Lord had given in the course of our courtship and over the course of our marriage, the many things we had accomplished together, the many things left to be accomplished…

Eddie passed away on Sunday, July 25th, on the day that Christians set aside for gathering to worship the Lord. He was called on that most appropriate day to worship Him in a fuller, better way, and to be with Him in eternity. It was a bittersweet day for all who loved him so. It was especially bittersweet for me, but especially sweet because of the time we had just spent together—time that God foresaw and foreordained to allow me to heal fully in His time, and to tell the story so that others can heal as well.

Praise be to the God and Father of our Lord Jesus Christ, the Father of compassion and the God of all comfort, who comforts us in all our troubles, so that we can comfort those in any trouble with the comfort we ourselves have received from God. For just as the sufferings of Christ flow over into our lives, so also through Christ our comfort overflows. If we are distressed, it is for your comfort and salvation; if we are comforted, it is for your comfort, which produces in you patient endurance of the same sufferings we suffer.
1 Cor. 1:3-6

During his five-month illness, Eddie did experience great discomfort but, praise the Lord, seldom excruciating pain. One that I admired the most is that he hardly ever complained—even at the end of his days.

Two years before his illness my dear husband had given me an alabaster box filled with the most hauntingly beautiful, fragrant oils. On the Sunday morning of his passing, I went home from the hospital, got the alabaster box, returned to the hospital and anointed his feet with the oils. It was 11:00 a.m. At 6:25 p.m. on that day, he was escorted into his heavenly home.

God had me in a "grace bubble." And there was no unfinished business between my dear husband, Rev. Eddie K.

Edwards and myself.

No more tears. And it is well with my soul.

When the death angel takes away someone we love, his or her last words seem so very, very important to us. Such was the case when I lost my dear husband in July 2004. The words spoken were not directly to me but about me.

During his illness, a pastor visited the hospital room. As the two of us sat beside my husband's bed, the pastor asked this question: *"What is it you like the most about your wife?"* As I sat there holding my breath, I quickly thought about all of the things I would like to hear him say. Since I've authored six books, it would have been nice to hear him say, *"Her creativity."* But, no, he didn't say that. Since I've been an ordained minister for over 20 years, it would have been nice to hear him say, *"Her prayer life or compassion for others."* But, no, he didn't say that. He didn't even agree with what so many others say is my greatest attribute: my infectious smile and wit. What he did say both surprised and disappointed me. *"Her strength,"* was his unexpected response.

I guess he could have said, *"I don't know."* That would have been an even bigger disappointment, not to mention the embarrassment I would have felt!

It's funny though how words that were once a disappointment to me have now become my greatest motivator as I go through life's many challenges. This is especially true those nights when I pull the covers over my head and cry myself to sleep. Then morning comes and I can hear my dear husband's words, *"Her strength."*

Although my wit isn't as quick, and my smile isn't as big as it used to be, remembering his words is the strength I need to get up, get out, and get going.

part two

Binding & Breaking Curses & Yokes

Since Eddie's death, I have given much thought to my family and the generations of challenges it has faced. In the second section of this book, I want to talk about one of our family strongholds: bipolarism. In the last chapter, I write a blessing to the people in my family. I pray that they receive and embrace it as so. I pray that those of you who read this will understand that transparency and honesty are the only ways to live, and that your family is your first and most important mission field.

Chapter 28

Widows With Wisdom

O death, where is thy sting? O grave, where is thy victory?
1 Cor. 15:55

Since the death angel took my husband away, I've given birth to a new baby: ***"Widows With Wisdom,"*** an outgrowth of *His Lovely Wife Ministries*. WWW is a support group for women such as myself who must learn how to live without their mates. Somehow I feel that my husband was preparing me for this moment in time, a moment that had many, many precursors.

In January of 2004, I began to meet some very interesting widows. They were older women with great wisdom. One of them was Mother Melissa Davis, a.k.a. "Mother Ruth." Mother Ruth was 93 years old at the time we met. I met Mother Ruth in a nail salon where she had a standing, that's right, standing appointment for every two weeks to get her fingers and toes groomed. Mother and I hit it off right away. I told her, *"Mother when I grow up I want to be just like you."* From that day to this, she calls me "Baby Ruth." Mother Ruth travels a great deal. Much of her travel is because she is sent for by large churches that want her to minister to them. Mother Ruth has outlived two husbands. The last time she got married she was 77 years old.

The second widow I met was Mother Ennis Byrdsong. Mother Byrdsong, age 85, has a perfect size 10 figure. She also has a personal fitness trainer and attends the fitness center at least twice a week. Mother Byrdsong is a nutrition specialist and takes absolutely no prescription medicines. She has written two books: her autobiography and a wonderful book on nutrition. Mother Byrdsong has a beau. He's 90 years old and she says he has perfect vision. Doesn't even need reading glasses, she says.

The third widow I met was Mother Ruthie Tate. Mother Tate came to me because she wanted to write a book. She was 79 at the time. Her birthday was coming up and she wanted to release her book by her 80th birthday, which she did. The title of her book is ***"God Made Morning Just For Me."*** She had her book signing at her 80th birthday party.

Needless to say, I found these widows to be intriguing. I was learning so much from them. So much so that in February 2004 I came home one day from visiting one of them and said to my husband, *"Somebody needs to start a ministry and name it Widows With Wisdom."* My husband and I laughed when he said, *"Well it won't be you. You're not a widow."* Needless to say, one month later he was diagnosed with fourth stage cancer. That was in March. In July he left for his heavenly home.

As I said in the beginning, God prepares us for the future. If we are tuned into His voice, nothing will surprise us. The Bible tells us that, if we are watchful and prayerful, nothing comes upon us unawares. I now know this, not from reading or hearing about it, but from personal experience.

Information about ***Widows With Wisdom*** support group meetings can be obtained from our website: www.widowswithwisdom.org.

Minister Mary Edwards Introduces…

"Widows With Wisdom"

"Pure and undefiled religion before God and the Father is this: To visit orphans and widows in their trouble, and to keep oneself unspotted from the world."

(James 1:27)

DATE:	Saturday, September 4, 2004
TIME:	1:00 p.m. – 3:00 p.m.
PLACE:	Mary's Home in Detroit, MI
RSVP:	(555) 555-5555

If you or someone you know is a widow, you are cordially invited to attend the launching of "Widows With Wisdom" (WWW). WWW is a support group whose mission is to educate, encourage, and embrace those who must learn how to make the adjustment to living without their spouse.

There were 15 women at that first meeting. We had a phenomenal time!

Following Eddie's departure, many people have asked, and perhaps even more have wondered, how I can be so peaceful about the loss. Well, like any other woman who has lost someone she loves and lived with for 21 years, a day doesn't go by that I don't miss him. What gives me great peace, however, is knowing that there wasn't any unfinished business between us when he went home to be with the Lord. God saw to that.

Is there something you need to do? If so, just do it —now! I followed that advice when I spent those last days with Eddie, and two short months later, I'm glad that I followed that advice again.

Also following Eddie's departure, I found something I had written many, many years before—before, even, I married Eddie. Now, I realize that it was written to prefigure what had transpired on September 4, 2004, the first official meeting of WWW:

MY COCOON

Written: June 28, 1981

Recently my niece April gave me a gift that is worth more to me than silver and gold. She gave me three caterpillars in a glass jar containing some tree bark and tumbleweed.

No monetary value can be placed on this gift because of the tremendous lessons God has taught me each time I pick up this jar and gaze at my specimens. Truly God has spoken to me from this jar, just as He did to Moses from the burning bush.

When I first received my gift, all three of the caterpillars were alive and two of them moved about at a moderate pace. However, the third one seemed to have an oversupply of nervous energy. Initially, all three would continuously climb to the top of the jar and try to escape through the rugged and sharply pierced holes. And I was fearful that they would be hurt trying to get out. However, after a relatively short period of time, two of the caterpillars, whom I will call April and May, ceased their struggle, began to fade in color, and formed a cocoon around their bodies. The cocoons were so ugly that at first I thought the caterpillars were dead, but a very close inspection revealed that there was yet slight movement inside of the enclosure.

Now, let us focus for a while on the third caterpillar, June. June is the one that never stopped moving about. If I got up in the middle of the night, June was on the move. Morning and noon as well, June was racing from the top of the jar to the bottom. She would even pick at April and May who had already entered into their cocoons.

If June ever rested, I am not aware of it. Alas, now she is at the bottom of the jar. You must look hard to see her for she is caught up among the weeds and still in her natural state. She isn't moving. I believe she is dead. What a shame that she had to die to get some rest.

Today, as I sit holding my jar, the Lord is yet speaking and I can hear the Voice of Jesus saying:

"Come unto me and rest. Cease from thy own works
and labor to enter into my rest. So many of my people are
struggling, trying to get away, when I would that they be still
and know that I am God. You don't have to provide your own
methods of escape for I will do that for you in due season.
When you try to escape through man's devices,
it will be likened unto the rugged and sharp holes in
the top of this jar and you will not be able to escape without
getting hurt. If you continue to struggle, you will end up as
June did. June struggled with her last breath to escape.
Now she is tangled up in the weeds on the bottom of the jar.
The cares of this word have choked the life out of her.
"But, if you cast your cares upon me and be anxious
for nothing, if you learn to be content in whatsoever
state you are in, if you labor to enter into my rest, you
will be as April and May. April and May are resting in Me.
I, too, have a cocoon just for you who are weary from your
journey. My cocoon is the secret place of the Most High God.
Abide in Me. Get away from it all. My cocoon will
provide refuge for your soul. My cocoon cannot be
penetrated by the cares of this world. My cocoon is more
durable than an iron fortress. My cocoon will keep
out the noisome pestilence. My cocoon will keep out
all the fiery darts of the devil. In my cocoon, you
will find safety against destruction. In my cocoon, you
will develop from a silkworm into a beautiful butterfly.
The walls of my cocoon are even more precious than
the silk that makes up this cocoon.
Yea, you will mount up with wings and fly."

THUS SAITH THE LORD

~

Two years after Eddie's death, and fifteen years after penning "My Cocoon," I wrote another piece. It's similar to cocoon, but written from a decidedly different perspective:

God's "Grace Bubble"

As I write this, I am approaching the second anniversary of my dear husband's transition to his heavenly home on July 25, 2004. His soul is resting in peace. And so is mine. It's all because of God's Grace Bubble. I won't say that this transition has been easy for me but, because of God's Grace Bubble, more things are going right than going wrong.

Every morning when I arise I say, *"Lord, order my steps in your Word today."* And He does. Let me give you a few examples that I hope will help you understand the Grace Bubble.

Prior to Rev. Edwards' departure, we had plans to move to Texas and had a lot of Texas clothing: hats, boots, jeans, etc. Well, after Rev. passed, it was hard for me to wear any of this clothing. However, one day not long after his departure, I prepared to dress. Very clearly, I heard the Lord say, *"Put on your Texas garb."* So I did, and left home headed for the post office.

Upon arriving at the U.S. Post Office and opening the box, there was only one little envelope inside. Had there been more mail, it could have easily been lost inside of one of the papers. Then, again, it couldn't have been lost because it was a very special card. This is how it read: *"Sorry, cowgirl, you lost your cowboy."* My knees nearly buckled! Here I stood dressed in my western clothing and reading this sympathy note from someone I didn't know! I was determined to find out who this person was.

Immediately, I went back home and called Information to see if I could get a phone number for my sympathizer. Fortunately, the spelling of the name was unusual and I got the number and called. The lady on the other end, Rose McGhee, told me how we had met. It was at a ladies' convention in Nashville, Tennessee, the year before. In a small group of ladies, I mentioned that my husband and I were going to move to Texas and be a cowboy and a cowgirl. When she heard that my husband had passed, she remembered our conversation. She had my business card and dropped her God-inspired card in the mail. That made my day. Just to know how God was watching over me and knew just what I needed is more than I can express.

Lord, how great Thou art! He had me dress for the occasion, and then He sent words of comfort to me through someone I didn't even know. This is just one example of God's Grace Bubble. Let me give you another one.

God often speaks to me in the shower. This is a place where He rains His shower of love down on me in the beginning of my day, following the reading of His word and prayer. Well, one morning He spoke to me and said: *"Mary, because you have given so many people a new start in life, (that was the name of my ministry in the Joy of Jesus family life program) I'm going to give you a new start in life."*

Later that same day I opened up one of the sympathy cards that were steadily coming to my home. The one I want to tell you about had a cross on the outside and the words,

"God Bless You" on the front. When I opened up the card the words inside said, *"Happy Birthday."* The handwritten words on the bottom said, *"We're praying for you."* This couple probably grabbed the card hastily and thought it was a sympathy card. But I know differently. God had them send that card to confirm that He was going to give me a new start in life. Isn't that what a birthday is?

There is so much more that I could say to let you know how the Lord has been blessing me for the past two years. But I'll save it for another day.

God has a Grace Bubble for you also. His grace is sufficient for whatever you may be going through.

Chapter 29

What Is Bipolarism?

Family shame is a dangerous thing. It keeps us from exposing our problems, and therefore from addressing them.

God often speaks to me in parables. A parable is a simple story told to illustrate a moral truth. To help me better understand the mental illnesses that have plagued my family, God gave me the following "real life" parable:

In one week, three light bulbs burned out in the socket on my front porch. Each time this happened, I replaced the bulb. Finally, it dawned on me that perhaps it wasn't the bulb, but the socket it was screwed into. Perhaps it was faulty wiring? This proved to be true when I tested the last bulb that "blew out" in a different socket. It worked fine. Unfortunately, I discarded the other two bulbs without first testing to see what the problem was. I assumed it was the bulb's fault.

Likewise, society and more specifically, families too often cast aside a troubled family member without taking the time to get to the root of the problem, or they deny its very existence. I have seen this happen over and over again in my family.

Let's deal with the issue of denial for a moment. It's called the "Elephant in the living room syndrome." Now, you and I both know it's impossible to ignore a big old elephant in the middle of the living room. With it, you'd be hard pressed to see out of the window, to see the television, or to see each other. It can also be embarrassing when friends come to visit! What do you do with the elephant? Put a doily on top of it and pretend it doesn't exist? Heaven forbid if it should rear up and knock a hole in the roof or trample all over you—or your friends! Nevertheless, families continue to pretend it doesn't exist. But ignoring it won't make it go away.

The mental illness known as "bipolar disease" is a big elephant in any family's living room. To complicate this particular issue, bipolar people frequently have other illnesses, along with this condition. It's called a "dual diagnosis." That is certainly true in my family, where those diagnosed with bipolarism were and are addicted to alcohol as well as prescription and non-prescription drugs. My late sister was never medically diagnosed, but she took Anacin everyday, all day, *"just in case I get a headache,"* she would tell me. Few in my family drink whiskey, but they sure can drink some beer. Tragically, some of them saw their money literally go up in smoke as they blew it away in the crack pipe.

Perhaps by now you are wondering, *"What is bipolarism?"* Good question. Simply put, even though this is not a simple disease, bipolarism is a condition in which the person affected suffers from both depressive and "manic" episodes. He or she can feel very sad and down for some time, even days, and then become very happy, energetic, and hyperactive. Both conditions or emotional states are out of the person's control, triggered by both external (emotional) and internal (chemical-health) reasons. For this reason, a more common name for bipolarism is "manic depression."

Bipolarism can be treated with psychotherapy, conducted by a psychologist or a psychiatrist as well as with medication (that can only be prescribed by a psychiatrist). A combination of therapy and medication usually provides the best results.

Experts estimate that bipolarism affects about 6 million U.S. citizens; and that the disease has a hereditary connection, meaning it often runs in families. Chances are you have at least one family member affected by this very difficult yet treatable disease. Unfortunately, in our community—the African American community—we are stigmatized if we or a family member visits a therapist. You've heard the phrase, haven't you? "She's/he's not crazy; they just need to get their life together. All they need is a good talking-to by grandma, or Aunt Etta Mae, and they'll be alright." If, when grandma or Aunt Etta Mae talks to them, they're not alright, we sweep it under the rug, or just decide to let our loved one live with the condition. How tragic for them, and for us—and how unnecessary.

It's time for those of us who care to lay the axe to the root of this problem and involve ourselves in the treatment process. Later in this chapter I will show you how. But before that I want to share an interview with you that I had with a woman who suffered with bipolarism for years before it was identified and treated. My friend, whom I will call "M," has had a traumatic life. At the age of 21, she went into a treatment program for alcoholics. She has been sober for nearly 18 years. In her words, *"I drank to escape reality. I drank and once I started I could not stop. I was suicidal a few months before getting sober. My life got so much better after getting sober. But being mentally ill, I could not accept that sentence. I wish I would have been diagnosed with cancer or anything else but mental illness."*

We'll call her "M."

Interview with "M"

MARY: Have you been medically diagnosed? If so, when and at what age?

M: *Yes, I have been medically diagnosed bipolar. I was diagnosed on January 4, 1994. I was 26 years old.*

MARY: What prompted you to get the diagnosis?

M: *My father had passed away the year before which was very traumatic for me. He was also bipolar and was sick from the time I was three. There was also a Nor`easter storm in New York where I was living that flooded my apartment that same year. I had been diagnosed with Chronic Fatigue Syndrome and Epstein Barr virus [both conditions are considered difficult to diagnose because of the varied possible symptoms, including general pain and extreme fatigue, which are symptoms that can describe any number of other conditions.]. I believe there was a physical attack on my body that preceded my mental breakdown.*

I was first diagnosed when I was found at JFK airport trying to get in a secured area. I had managed to get on the tarmac because I was looking for my "private jet" that I believed was there.

MARY: What had you heard about bipolar disease before you were diagnosed?

M: *Before I was diagnosed bipolar I lived with my father who was first diagnosed schizophrenic in 1970 and later in the early 80's diagnosed bipolar. My father usually wore his pajamas and rarely went outside. He was heavily medicated his whole life. He made frequent trips to state run mental hospitals. It was a very scary place to me and so was the illness.*

MARY: How has the disease impacted the way you relate to your family/children?

M: *Thankfully I was diagnosed and put on medication at the first onset of my mania. Even though this was a very terrible and serious mania, I am thankful that up until today I have not had another manic episode. I continue to take my medicine and have found peace and healing through following Jesus Christ. Because of being saved through Jesus and called by name by God, I believe that I am stable. My faith has helped me. I do believe my medicine also helps me and I will probably continue to take it for the rest of my life. My family understands that I have been diagnosed with this disease but I am thankful they have yet to see me sick with the mania or depression of this illness.*

MARY: What medication are you taking?

M: *I take Lithium, which I started from the diagnosis of this illness. I also take Synthroid for my thyroid. I have hypothyroidism [an under-active thyroid, which can also cause fatigue].*

MARY: How are your family members taking it? Are they supportive?

M: *My mother is one of the strongest women I know. She has been through a lot with my father's illness. My husband is very loving and supportive. Even though he has never experienced mental illness in his own family, he tries to understand and has compassion. My children are still very young and I don't speak to them about this subject often but it does come up when I talk to them about my childhood and my father. Because I have been stable on medicine, I look like someone who is not affected with mental illness.*

MARY: Besides your father, are there other family members who are bipolar or suffer from other mental illnesses?

M: *My parents had five children. Four out of the five children, including me, have been diagnosed bipolar. All of us have full productive lives.*

MARY: Do you find yourself embarrassed to talk about this?

M: *Yes. When my father got sick, he was shunned by friends. People who were very close to my parents and godparents to us disowned our family. It was terrible the way they treated my dad. When I got sick I got the same response from "close friends." They looked at me differently and I got the sense that they thought if they got too close to me they would catch what I had. As I got older and more stable, I thought I could share my childhood memories. I did this with a woman I had met through my son's Christian school. I only shared with her my father's struggles in a general way. Afterwards, she wanted nothing to do with me or my son. This was just last year and I promised that I would never speak about mental illness and my personal experience with it with anyone. It was shortly after this that God burdened my heart with people who needed to hear my experience and I shared publicly about my mental illness.*

MARY: What strategies have helped you the most?

M: The strategy that has helped me the most is prayer, reading the Bible and taking my medicine. Also trying to be of service. It is when I am helping others that I feel most balanced and happy. I also keep a journal for my children so they can understand how God has carried our family through many difficulties. I also would like for them to see the miracles that God continues to bless us with; to see how His Hand has guided and protected us.

MARY: What have you learned that you could share with others—Practical matters as well as spiritual matters?

M: Paul says in 2 Corinthians 12:7, "To keep me from becoming conceited because of these surpassingly great revelations, there was given me a thorn in my flesh, a messenger of Satan, to torment me." I feel that we each have our own thorn. Mine happens to be bipolar. It reminds me that God has created me to have this for a reason. When I got sick I was put on disability, which I am grateful for because at the time I could not keep a job. Later though I tried to cancel my disability and was told by the State that they still believed me to be disabled. Even though I continued to try to cancel benefits it was never stopped. Then one day I called and told them I no longer wanted the money they were sending me for being disabled. I was told I needed to go to the office in person. When I went to the local Social Security office, they said that they have never had anyone want to stop benefits and wanted me to see their doctor. They finally stopped sending me money but my case still isn't closed. I used to view my illness and past with shame and remorse until God gave me the grace to see the freedom I have from it. I have bipolar but I am not disabled. And taking the money every month made some part of me believe that lie. Today, I know the truth and it has set me free. Today, I have a personal relationship with Jesus Christ and I want to share His glory and forgiveness and grace with others. Today, I am a child of the King, which makes me a princess and I wear my crown with dignity and pride. Today, I know that my experience and freedom needs to be shared publicly so the "stigma" of mental illness doesn't kill the people still chained. Today, I have a voice that will speak for the people who cannot speak. Today, I am free and pray for that freedom for all prisoners of mental illness.

MARY:	Are you familiar with the National Association of Mental Illness (NAMI)? If so, what has been your experience with them?
M:	*Yes. Right after I got out of the mental hospital 13 years ago I went to a NAMI meeting. I felt very discouraged because the only people that were there were family members of people with bipolar disease or people who were very sick and heavily sedated. It was actually very depressing. I believe that at that time people who had mental illness and were living productive lives didn't go to the meetings. I am currently seeking to get to meetings in my area so I may be able to offer hope to someone who may be just coming out of the hospital like I was 13 years ago.*
MARY:	Do you have any other comments you wish to make?
M:	*Yes. Before I got sick I had been sober for five years. I loved life. I was starting to make a name for myself. I also was starting to read the Bible. After I got sick, it was like my life ended. People treated me differently. I had lost my love of life and wanted to die. I did not want to wind up like my dad. I did not want to end up alone. I didn't think anyone would want to be my friend since I had lost so many when I got sick. Even my best friend at the time said she couldn t visit me in the hospital because it was too much for her. I didn't think anyone would want to marry me either. I felt like one of those misfit toys in Rudolf the*

	Red-Nosed Reindeer. I felt like no one would want to love me. I poured some pills in my hand in hopes of taking my life. I just couldn't bear being mentally ill. I had seen how people treated my dad and I just knew I wasn't strong enough for that persecution. That is when God met me. He lifted me up and has carried me from that day to this. I told God I wasn't strong enough to live and He has answered me with Isaiah 41:10: "So do not fear, for I am with you; do not be afraid for I am your God. I will strengthen you. I will help you. I will hold you by my righteous right hand." I am so thankful that God is so faithful.
MARY:	Thank you so much for your willingness to share such a deeply moving testimony. Many people will be helped because of your boldness to be transparent. God bless you, my friend.

Chapter 30

An Open Letter to My Family

The eternal God is your refuge, and underneath are the everlasting arms. Deut. 33:27

The word of the Lord says that Jesus Christ was a man of sorrow and acquainted with grief (Isa. 53:3); and that He was moved with compassion and touched by our infirmities (Heb. 4:15). Likewise, I have felt the pain that all of you have suffered over the years. The physical pain of various diseases, such as cancer; the emotional pain of bipolarism and other mental illnesses; and the spiritual pain that comes from personally experiencing the sins of the world and not having the Lord Jesus Christ as the center of your lives.

The Bible says that the sins of the fathers are visited upon their children for up to four generations (Ex. 20:5). In case you are not familiar with that scripture, let me put it to you this way: what the parents did in moderation the children will do in excess. As I look at our family tree, this has proven to be true. However, I have spoken the Word of God over your lives and believe with all my heart that it will come to pass.

Here, then: the meanings of all of your names:

My Son, Darrell: "Beloved One; Blessed One."
Supporting Scripture: Psalm 18:32(KJV) –
"It is God that girdeth me with strength,
and maketh my way perfect."

My son, Donald: "Courageous heart; Compassion"
Supporting Scripture: James 2:22 (NIV)
"You see, his faith (Abraham) and his actions
were working together, and his faith was made
complete by what he did."

My grandson, Darrell, Jr.: "Beloved One; Blessed One
Supporting Scripture: Psa. 18:32
"It is God that girdeth me with strength,
and maketh my way perfect."

My granddaughter, Eboni (Danielle):
Ebony means dark. I'm going to give you the
biblical meaning of your middle name "Danielle."
It is the feminine form of the name Daniel,
the great man in the Bible who had incredible

powers of discernment and wisdom beyond
his chronological age (Dan. 2:19-23).
Danielle: "Spiritual Judgment; Spiritual Discernment.
Supporting Scripture: Ps. 119:112
"I have inclined my heart to perform thy
statues always, even until the end."

My grandson, Jason: "Healer; Quickened in Spirit"
Supporting Scripture: Luke 6:45
"A good man, out of the good treasure of
his heart, bringeth forth that which is good."

My granddaughter, Jasmyne:
"Jasmine Flower; Messenger of Love"
Supporting Scripture: Isa. 55:11
"So shall my word be that goeth forth out of
my mouth, it shall not return unto me void,
But it shall accomplish that which I please, and
it shall prosper in the thing whereto I sent it."

My niece, Rachel: "Innocence, Gentleness, Blessed One"
Supporting Scripture: Hosea 14:9
"Who is wise, and he shall understand
these things? Prudent, and he shall know them?
For the ways of the Lord are right, and the just
shall walk in them…"

My niece, April (Dawn) – "New in faith; Awakened soul"

Supporting Scripture: Ezek. 37:14

"And I shall put my spirit in you and ye
shall live, and I shall place you in your own land:
then shall ye know that I the Lord have spoken it,
and performed it..."

Dawn: "Beginning anew; Joy and praise"

Supporting Scripture: Psalm 113:2-3

"Blessed be the name of the Lord from this
time forth and forevermore. From the rising
of the sun unto the going down of the same the
Lord's name is to be praised."

Epilogue

Family, I pray you are blessed by my story, and by the many experiences that I have so openly shared with you. I pray that we break the generational curses that plague us, and that we begin an upward cycle of generational blessings to take their place. I leave you with these words of encouragement from our God. Yes, He is the God of all of us, because He made us and loves us so. Know this: we are being watched by God. Watched by our children and our children's children. And watched by the world.

Therefore, since we are surrounded by such a great cloud of witnesses, let us throw off everything that hinders and the sin that so easily entangles, and let us run with perseverance the race marked out for us. Let us fix our eyes on Jesus, the author and perfecter of our faith...Consider him who endured such opposition from sinful men, so that you will not grow weary and lose heart.

Heb. 12:1-2a, 3

And finally, to let you know that, because there are generational curses, God also provides as a remedy generational blessings:

I, the Lord your God,...[will show] love to a thousand generations, of those who love me and keep my commandments.
Ex. 20:5

While in the process of writing my personal history, there were many unpleasant things I had to record. Some of them relate to the women in my family—me included. Some of the details caused me to fall on my face and repent for my ancestors, as well as myself. I was pretty discouraged until the Holy Spirit brought to my attention that there were four notorious women in the official family tree of Jesus (Matt. 1:1-16): Tamar, Rahab, Ruth, and Bathsheba.

TAMAR: *She seduced her father-in-law to get pregnant.*
RUTH: *She wasn't even Jewish and broke the law by marrying a Jewish man.*
RAHAB: *She was a prostitute.*
BATHSHEBA: *She committed adultery with David, which resulted in her husband's murder.*

"Although my natural father never laid eyes on me, my Heavenly Father has never taken His eyes off me. The orphan spirit is gone...And I know what it is to be called "Daddy's girl." If Jesus could make it through—and He did—I guess I can! With His help, it's a done deal!

Love Him, family. Love Him more than your own life, your own dreams. Love Him more than the sins that keep you from His presence. And know that He loves you more than you could ever love even yourself. He loves you more, and better, than I ever will be able to love you. And I love you all deeply!

Love,

Ma, Mom, Grammy,

Grandma Darlene, Sis,

Auntie, Mary, Darlene,

and most of all,

Child of the King!

about the author

Minister Mary Edwards is probably best known for her community revitalization work alongside of her late husband Rev. Eddie K. Edwards. Together they founded the Joy of Jesus Ministries, which is located on the eastside of Detroit near City Airport. This work earned them the *107th Point of Light Award* from former President George W. Bush, Sr. Minister Edwards was the founding director of Camden House, the family life center of the ministry. As a result of this successful outreach, she was chosen to serve as a consultant to the advisory team in our nation's capital commissioned to study the *"Root Cause of Substance Abuse."*

In 1996, Minister Edwards retired from Joy of Jesus and began new initiatives. These include:

- *His Lovely Wife Ministries*, a support group for women in spiritual leadership

- *The Called and Ready Writers*, a Christian writers guild presently consisting of over 55 active writers.

- *Widows With Wisdom* (WWW), her latest ministry, established to help widows make the adjustment to living alone following the loss of their spouses. WWW is an outreach of *His Lovely Wife Ministries.*

Minister Edwards is the radio show host of "Widows With Wisdom" heard every Saturday morning at 9:00 a.m. over Radio Station WLQV (1500 AM) in Livonia, Michigan.

In addition to these ministries, Minister Edwards has authored six other books including her most cherished book which is titled, *Ponderings From the Heart of Mary*. Her late husband, Rev. Eddie K. Edwards, painted the cover. A significant testimony from her autobiography appears in the very first *Chicken Soup for the African American Soul* book released in September of 2004. She is an international author and speaker.

Minister Edwards is the mother of two sons, four grandchildren, and three great-grandchildren. You will often hear her quote the scripture from Prov. 13:22,"*A good man leaveth an inheritance to his children's children; and the wealth of the sinner is laid up for the just.*"

Minister Edwards believes in leaving a legacy behind.

BORN GROWN RESOURCES

BOOKS

Hickey, Marilyn, Break the Generation Curse Part 1 and Part 2, (Denver, Colorado: Marilyn Hickey Ministries, 1997). ISBN 1-56441-028-5

Stone, Perry, The Meal That Heals.(Cleveland, Tennessee, Voice of Evangelism Ministries, Inc., 2006) ISBN 0-9708611-8-4

Hagerman, Nancy L., In The Pit: A testimony of God's faithfulness to a bipolar Christian. (Belleville, Ontario, Canada, Essence Publishing, 2001
ISBN I-55306-200-0

Campbell, 72 Hour Hold. (New York, Alfred A. Knopf, © 2004, by ELMA, Inc.) ISBN 1-4000-40744-4

Price, Derek, Blessing or Curse: You Can Choose, Amazon.com

Find in a Library: Martin, Marilyn, Saving Our Last Nerve: the Black woman's path to mental health. (Hilton Publishing, 2002. ISBN 096752587x978096752877

MOVIE

"A Beautiful Mind" is an Academy Award-winning film inspired by the Nobel Peace Prize (Economics) winning mathematician John Nash and his experiences of schizophrenia. The film is loosely based on the more factual biography of the same name, which was written by Sylvia Nash and published in 1998.

ORGANIZATIONS

National Alliance for the Mentally Ill (NAMI)

Mental Illness Research Association (MIRA)

Dr. Lisa H. Fuller
Author, *You Already Have All of the Tools that You Need*
Psychiatrist, International Speaker
LRHF Mental Health Consultants, Executive Director
Learn Realistic Habits for the Future Publishing, President
P.O. Box 401259
Redford, MI 48240
(313) 645-1596
drlisafuller@aol.com
www.drlisafuller.com